'With sparkling passion for the gospel, Michael Green takes us on an a high-speed dash through the pages of revival history. From the Roman Empire, to Georgian England, to Communist China, here are perceptive lessons about the power of God to awaken the church both yesterday and today.'

Andrew Atherstone, tutor in history, Wycliffe Hall, Oxford

'Michael Green leads us through the history of some remarkable examples of revival both here in the UK, and across the world, and identifies the similar conditions that seem to come before revival. Those who hunger to see God move afresh in this generation should read this book.'

Amy Orr-Ewing, OCCA and UK Director of
RZIM Zacharias Trust

When God Breaks In

Revival can happen again

Michael Green

HODDER

First published in Great Britain in 2014 by Hodder & Stoughton
An Hachette UK company

This paperback edition first published in 2015

1

Copyright © Michael Green, 2014

A CIP catalogue record for this title is available from the British Library

ISBN 978 1 444 78795 5
eBook ISBN 978 1 444 78797 9

Typeset in Swift LT Std by Hewer Text UK Ltd, Edinburgh

Printed and bound in the UK by Clays Ltd, St Ives plc

Hodd   , renewable
and rec   nable forests.
The   conform
                                                        igin.

Contents

Foreword

W e are in a fascinating yet paradoxical situation. On one hand, worldwide secularisation appears to be proceeding apace. On the other, passionate belief in God is growing all over the world — with the exception of Western Europe. What are we to make of this apparent contradiction?

Again, on one hand many Christians in the West are discouraged by the waning of belief, and have ceased to expect God's intervention to change the situation. On the other hand, history reveals that time and again, when the spiritual outlook is bleakest, there are notable revivals of the gospel — revivals that have changed the course of entire nations.

This book is written to surprise sceptics, who think Christianity is on the way out, and to encourage Christians, not least in Britain, to believe that God is in business and well able to transform today's decline. Though the examples I choose to illustrate this theme are inevitably selective, such is the quantity of material available, this book aims to showcase some outstanding examples of renewal, from past history and the present day, both in the West and in the East — supremely, modern China. And most of all, it sets out to ignite the torch of hope that *God can do it again.*

Michael Green
Wycliffe Hall
Oxford University

1

Give me the springs!
Thirst for God

God is Back is the title of the book on my desk. This is not, as you might imagine, the hopeful cry of some religious enthusiast, but a substantial and carefully researched book by two writers who I think would call themselves atheists, John Micklethwait and Adrian Wooldridge. Next to it lies *The Desecularisation of the World* edited by perhaps the most distinguished sociologist alive today, Peter Berger.

What on earth is happening?

The resurgence of religion

The answer is that the most assured assumption of sociology has been shown to be completely wrong! Egg is on many a social scientist's face! Ever since the French Revolution it has been assumed that the advance of modernisation would inevitably mean the decline of religion. Sixty years ago it was an article of faith among sociologists that religion would fade away by about the year 2000. Peter Berger himself was pre-eminent among them in predicting the demise of religion, and now he cheerfully eats his words and admits he had got it completely wrong. 'The assumption that we live in a secularised world is false. The world today . . . is as furiously religious as it ever was, and in some places more so than ever.' He charmingly continues: 'As I like to tell my students, one advantage of being a social scientist . . . is that you can have as much fun when your theories are falsified as when they are verified.'

The truth of the matter is that belief in God is not only proving impossible to eradicate: worldwide, it is growing apace. Pentecostalism, for instance, emerged only a century or so ago, but already has over 500 million adherents worldwide. Africa is another example of massive Christian growth. At the start of the twentieth century there were fewer than ten million Christians in the whole of Africa. Now there are some 450 million! There are about two billion Christians in the world, increasing at a rapid pace, matched by the advance in numbers and confidence by some 800 million Muslims. The Jews are holding firm, and there is significant growth in Buddhism and Hinduism as well. It is estimated that the four biggest religions of the world, Christianity, Islam, Hinduism and Buddhism, accounted for 67 per cent of the world's population in 1900 and a hundred years later had grown to 73 per cent, and rising.

This may be part of the reason for the increasing stridency of the new atheists in the West, men like Sam Harris, Richard Dawkins and the late Christopher Hitchens. Could it be that they suspect that their basic assumption may be false, so they shout louder? Religion shows no sign whatever of dying in a world of advancing sophistication. For all the self-confidence you can detect in their writings, and their scorn of believers, the fact remains that they are in a tiny minority. Atheists constitute a microscopic proportion of the world's population.

Indeed, Dawkins, who boasts of being the most famous atheist alive, gets mentioned only twice in one of the books I mentioned above and not at all in the other. Both books are fascinated by the continual growth and dynamism of religion, particularly fundamentalist Islam and evangelical Christianity. Berger playfully alludes to the millions of dollars spent by the MacArthur Foundation on research into fundamentalism, as though passionate religious faith was hard to understand. He suggests that the money would have been better spent researching into why the subculture of academics, media moguls and politicians find religious conviction so hard to understand!

As you look round the religious map of the world it is not only the numbers that are arresting, but the willingness of adherents to stand firm for their beliefs in the face of opposition and persecution. And although this growth is a populist movement, particularly among poor people in Africa and Latin America, there is today a vigorous intellectual resurgence in defence of faith, among both evangelical Christians and Muslims, while politically the influence of religion is everywhere to be seen. There would have been no war in Iraq or Afghanistan had not nineteen Muslims killed themselves for their faith in attacking the Twin Towers in 2001. The same is true of almost all the trouble spots in the world — Israel, Pakistan, Nigeria, Indonesia. Sometimes, of course, religion forges peace, as it has between Christians and Muslims in Tanzania. But on any showing, religion is a massive factor to be reckoned with in human affairs.

Everywhere except Western Europe

There is one exception to the growing influence of religion — Western Europe. This was the birthplace of the eighteenth-century Enlightenment with its twin beliefs in human reason and human goodness. Here alone the old theory that modernisation leads to the death of religion seems to hold, though why the developed countries of Europe should be so godless whereas the even more developed country of the United States should be so god-fearing is problematic. But the fact remains: Europe in general and Britain in particular seem to have outgrown their Christian heritage.

The Christian faith used to be the dominant worldview in Europe, although of course a good deal of that will have been nominal. At all events, the majority of the population went to church. Christian ethics was the norm, whether you were a Christian or not. Christian education was taught in the schools. Many homes would have family prayers. The laws were framed on broadly Christian standards. The majority of people would have called themselves Christians, whether or not it meant much to them.

What a transformation today! Within two or three generations, and at an accelerating pace, it is all change. Church attendance in Britain is down to some 5 per cent, and despite the historic bedrock of Christianity underpinning so many of our institutions, Christianity has become a minority faith in the country. Many clergy have never seen anybody, let alone any adult, convert to the Christian faith. A great many churches are virtually deserted. Most have no youth work at all, and countless youngsters have never entered a church building. Little is taught about Christianity in the schools, for they are committed to a multi-faith approach. A meagre smattering of information about some of the main religions is given, often taught by staff who do not believe any of them.

Few young families and fewer working men attend worship: church is seen to be the preserve of middle-class people over seventy. Great swathes of the country have no knowledge of even the basics of Christianity. Christmas is seen as a spending spree, involving excessive consumption, and Easter means chocolate rabbits.

Their origin in the coming, the dying and the rising of the man who split history in two is forgotten.

Within the Church the decline is no less apparent. Even among regular churchgoers belief in the historic facts of Christianity is sketchy, and for many, family prayers and Bible reading have disappeared. Church members have no enthusiasm for spreading the faith, owing to the prevalent rejection of religion in society. The money given to support overseas missionary work is microscopic, though church people do join fully with people of other faiths and none in humanitarian action in the face of natural disasters, seeking to rectify homelessness, and running food banks. But when you look for deep habits of prayer, clear understanding of the faith, passion for evangelism and firm ethical standards − qualities which have been associated with lively Christianity down the centuries − they are often hard to find in today's Church.

Society at large is no longer influenced by Christian belief and standards of behaviour. The norms of our legal system are no longer determined by the Bible but by the human rights legislation administered by Brussels, which came in after the Second World War in an effort to prevent any repetition of Nazi atrocities. Abortion on demand has become a major industry − 200,000 a year in the UK alone. Homosexual activity, although clearly forbidden in the Bible, is increasingly accepted as normal, despite the massive health risks involved, and as I write there is worldwide vilification of Russia, which does not allow homosexual practice to be taught to minors. The very nature of marriage, universally recognised in the world as being between a man and a woman, has been re-invented to enable two men or two women to marry — and the age of consent has been reduced to sixteen. Divorce and fornication have long since been normalised, and I have heard on the BBC the next step in sexual permissiveness being touted — polygamy and polyandry.

Not to put too fine a point on it, Christianity is in low water. God is left entirely out of account by most Europeans, and laughed out of court by many. Atheism is more fashionable than at any time in our history. The very concept of right and wrong has largely disappeared. In our postmodern society the best we can do is to say, 'It seems right to me but of course it may seem very different to you.' There are no objective standards. Truth itself has run into the sands of subjectivism and relativism. Truth claims are seen as power games. It is time for the Church to wake up.

Sleeper, awake!

In ancient Ephesus you would have heard some of the slaves singing it; you would have noticed some of the errand boys whistling it. 'Wake up, sleeper, rise from the dead, and Christ will shine on you.' This was one of the early Christian songs, and the apostle Paul alludes to it in his letter to the church at Ephesus (5:14). If ever the cry of 'Wake up, sleeper!' was needed, it is imperative today if the Church and Christian civilisation are to survive.

Do not imagine that I am pessimistic about the future of Christianity. Nothing could be further from my mind. Did not Jesus predict that the gates of hell would not be able to prevail against the advance of the kingdom? Nor have they! Time and again down the past two thousand years Christians have been persecuted, tortured and slaughtered. Their holy book has been consigned to the flames. They have been forbidden to allow the name of Jesus to pass their lips. Society has ostracised them, written them off, laughed at them and killed them. But the gospel continues to grow, particularly in countries where it has never been strong before. A graphic modern example is China, as we shall see in a later chapter. When the missionaries were kicked out in 1952 there were perhaps five million Christians in that great land. Now the estimate is that there are probably in the region of a hundred million, and they appear to be growing at a rate of some twenty thousand a day. No, the gospel will not die, but national churches and denominations may. So it is always important for Christians to heed the call to wake up, and remember that the Church is always only one generation away from extinction.

It is helpful to look back at times in the past when the spiritual outlook seemed bleak, but then God broke through in a remarkable way and transformed the situation. I propose to look at a number of such occasions in this book. The Old Testament book of Judges is a useful pointer. It shows how the people of Israel were so often lawless and apostate, but in generation after generation, when all seemed lost, they turned back to God and cried to him for deliverance. And each time he raised up a 'saviour' for them — men like Gideon or Samson — who became God's agent in restoration. The patience and humility of God is breathtaking. People can spit in his eye, swear he does not exist and yet, when they reach the end of their tether and reluctantly turn to him as the last forlorn hope, he breaks in and comes triumphantly to their aid.

It has been like that with the history of Christianity in Britain and beyond. In the pages that follow I want to trace some of those divine renewals, majoring on Britain, because they will bring encouragement that God can do it again. They will also give us some examples of the human conditions that appear to be needed before we can expect God to act. These may enable us to 'wake up, and rise from the dead', and in his mercy 'Christ will shine on us'.

It is at first sight strange that this early Christian song should call on us first to wake up and then to rise from the dead. But surely there are two categories in mind here, the sleeping and the dead. And those two categories exist in many of our churches! There is a massive amount of ability, skill and dynamism in the pews, but it is largely somnolent. It has not been mobilised. It needs to wake up to the social and political mire by which we are engulfed as a result of our spiritual apostasy. The Church is dominated by its ministers to far too great an extent. Laypeople are often not encouraged to take initiative. Instead they are corralled into being mini-clergy, taking the collection, being sidespeople, running children's meetings and perhaps preaching occasionally in church. It is not often that you see a coordinated plan to mobilise the congregation as a whole to serve the local community in whatever way is appropriate. We need to wake up! Christians need to get involved and to speak up in sport, politics, social concerns, the media, academia — the places where decisions are made and policy formulated.

But there are others in our churches who are not just asleep but spiritually dead. I recall a distinguished Roman Catholic, Cardinal Suenens, leading a mission in Oxford University some years ago, and referring to the many thousands of 'baptised pagans' in Europe. Some of the college chaplains walked out in high dudgeon, but he was perfectly right. Baptism is the mark of the new birth but it cannot confer it. Only God can do that. Just as we need to experience natural birth if we are to be humans at all, so we need to experience spiritual birth if we are to be Christians at all. It is indispensable. Yet in many churches you hear nothing of the need for a radical new beginning, a new birth, as the New Testament calls it. It is assumed that if you have been baptised and if you come to church from time to time you must be a Christian, whether you believe the Christian faith or not. But that is crazy, and the apostles will have none of it. 'You were dead in your transgressions and sins,' writes Paul to these same Ephesians to whom he included this little chorus: 'Wake up, sleeper, rise from the dead.'

You were dead in your transgressions and sins, in which you used to live . . . All of us also lived among them at one time, gratifying the cravings of our flesh and following its desires and thoughts. Like the rest, we were by nature deserving of wrath. But because of his great love for us, God, who is rich in mercy, made us alive with Christ even when we were dead in transgressions – it is by grace you have been saved.

(Ephesians 2:1:5)

From spiritual death to spiritual life – that is the essential and astonishing transformation which describes every true Christian. So the 'dead' need to come to the Lord for new life, in our day as in the first century. And the 'sleepers' need the wake-up call which will jolt them into action. 'Wake up, sleeper, rise from the dead, and Christ will shine on you.'

Give me the springs!

A South African cardiologist and Christian leader, Dr Khalid Leon, has drawn my attention to a couple of remarkable but usually unnoticed passages in the Old

11

Testament about water. Water is of priceless value in a hot country where much of the land is desert, and accordingly water figures largely in both the Old Testament and the New. It is a symbol of spiritual life. When Isaiah paints the picture of what return from exile could mean for the Jews, he hears God saying

The poor and needy search for water, but there is none; their tongues are parched with thirst. But I the LORD will answer them; I, the God of Israel, will not forsake them. I will make rivers flow on barren heights, and springs within the valleys. I will turn the desert into pools of water, and the parched ground into springs.

(Isaiah 41:17:18)

And who can forget that remarkable interview between Jesus and the woman of Samaria about her need to draw physical water from the well, and her hunger for spiritual water which Jesus himself could provide? Water in the Bible is a central symbol of spiritual vitality.

That lends a fascinating emphasis to Genesis 26:18, where we read, 'Isaac reopened the wells that had been dug in the time of his father Abraham, which the Philistines had stopped up after Abraham died.' This was essential for Isaac if he and his family, his flocks and herds were to survive in that climate! But we must not miss the symbolism. In past centuries of Christianity, in Britain as elsewhere, some very significant wells have been dug, but over the course of time they have been blocked off with all sorts of rubble, sometimes by opponents and sometimes by the slovenliness of the Church. They need to be reopened, if we are to regain the fresh, cooling water. 'Everyone who drinks this water will be thirsty again,' said Jesus to the woman of Samaria. 'But whoever drinks the water I give them will never thirst. Indeed, the water I give them will become in them a spring of water welling up to eternal life.' No wonder the urgent cry of the woman was, 'Sir, give me this water so that I won't get thirsty' (John 4:13ff).

That cry is anticipated in the Old Testament. The patriarch Caleb gave some of the land that was his inheritance to his daughter Aksah and her husband Othniel.

One day . . . when she got off her donkey, Caleb asked her, 'What can I do for you?' She replied, 'Do me a special favour. Since you have given me land in the Negev, give me also springs of water.' So Caleb gave her the upper and lower springs.

(Judges 1:14-15)

This incident was significant enough to be repeated in the very same words in Joshua 15:17-19. The Negev is desert. What use is land in the desert without springs of water? None at all. And what use are the mainline churches, with their denominations, their property, their pomp and circumstance, their learning and their politics, without divine renewing, the springs of living water? 'Give me the springs' was Aksah's plea. It might

13

well be ours, as we turn from the desert of what the
Church is to the fruitful land it could become if only
there was water. So in this book we shall look at several
significant occasions when God has given us deep wells,
but alas they have got clogged up and need reopening.
We will look at several times when springs of water
have burst out of the dry ground, and hopefully we will
covet and pray for something similar in our own day. I
hope it will stimulate Christian readers to cry to the
Lord, 'Give me the springs.'

2

A spring in the desert
Pentecost

If ever there was a crying need for God to break in, it was in the little land of Judaea in what we now call the first century AD.

God's preparation

For two thousand years God had been nurturing a people who would offer him pure worship, reflect something of his character and be a light to the nations. He began by finding a man, Abraham, who would trust him and follow him wholeheartedly. God promised to bless the whole world through his descendants. But that looked as if it would lead nowhere because Sarah his wife was barren. However, God intervened and miraculously she gave birth to Isaac, whose own son was Jacob, and from that family the people of Israel traced their descent.

But then disaster threatened. It looked as if they would all perish from starvation in one of the periodic famines that struck the Middle East. Could God handle that situation? He could. Once again there was an almost miraculous intervention, which showed that God had not given up on the Israelites. Joseph, Jacob's son, whom his brothers thought they had killed, turned up, to their amazement, as the right-hand man to the pharaoh, to whom they had journeyed hoping to buy grain. Joseph was in charge of administering the corn reserves of the whole of Egypt. Not only was there a moving reconciliation between the brothers, but Jacob and his whole extended family were invited to come and live in Egypt.

But then disaster struck again. The Israelites were getting too prosperous for the Egyptians' liking, and so they were reduced to slavery and the order went out to kill all their firstborn males. Surely that was the end of the story? Far from it. It was almost the beginning. God broke in once again, most dramatically, in the exodus. Israel made a successful escape from Egypt and the soldiers who were pursing them got drowned in the Red Sea. The next step should have been easy enough. They had only to cross the Sinai desert and ford the Jordan to enter the land which God had promised them. After all they had been through that did not seem too demanding. But once again they found themselves in trouble. Instead of a direct route, the Israelites wandered to and fro in the desert for a whole generation as God's punishment for their disobedience and lack of faith.

And when they did eventually get into the promised land, the story was not a stunning success. To be sure there were high points under leaders like David and Solomon, but pagan worship and idolatry persisted, the country split into two, and despite the prophets God sent to them on many occasions to call them back to his obedience, Israel's apostasy was so great that it needed a seventy-year exile in Babylon to bring them to their senses.

You might have thought that would have made priorities very plain, but not a bit of it. The people continued in idolatry and immorality, and so God allowed them to be overcome by foreign rulers for generations. It seemed that God had broken in once again in the second century BC with the emergence of the Maccabees, but their fantastic victory over Antiochus Epiphanes, the Syrian overlord, and their restoration of the Jewish religion proved short-lived. By the first century BC Israel was once again in a bad way under the control of Herod, a half-pagan despot. They were desperate for rescue from the Roman forces which stood behind Herod's client kingdom. Soon after his death the Romans would invade, and turn the country into a province of the empire.

Once again, God's plan looked like faltering. The land, though religious, was a spiritual desert, and the Jewish leadership was split into four opposing parties, all of them nurturing the hope of throwing the Romans out, but very divided on the method. The Essenes ran a monastic community in the desert, waiting for the 'day

17

of the Lord'. Then they would fight. The Pharisees eschewed military action but hoped that by punctilious observance of the law they could bring in the day of the Lord's victory. The Sadducees held their noses but voted to cooperate with the Romans until better times prevailed. And the nationalist zealots hung around on dark nights hoping to slit the throat of a careless Roman solder or two. It was a spiritual desert indeed. The question in many a faithful heart was surely this: could God break in again?

We all know the answer. It burst upon the world like a geyser of bright water gushing up in the desert. It was a stream that split all history into two, from BC to AD.

God's personal intervention

What happened was this. God determined that he would intervene in person both to show how human life ought to be lived and to set his people free from spiritual decay. The God of the unexpected chose Joseph, a builder, and Mary his young fiancée, as the agents of this world-shattering event. God impregnated Mary's womb and in due course Jesus was born. This may seem totally incredible, because nothing like it has ever happened before or since. But then God has never visited his world in person before or since. Hard though it is to believe, because of its wonder and uniqueness, it is nevertheless strongly attested in first- and second-century writers, and has won the faith of countless millions down the succeeding centuries. They have been persuaded of the divinity of Jesus by his matchless teaching, his perfect life, his love to one and all, his miracles, his fulfilment of many of the great prophecies of the Old Testament, his claims to forgive sins, to accept worship, to be the final judge of humankind and to be the way to God. His earliest followers, all Jewish monotheists who would have found the idea of incarnation utterly repugnant to their belief system, were gradually convinced. They were deeply impressed by these marks of Jesus' divinity, but they were finally persuaded by his death and resurrection that he was indeed what they called 'the Son of God'.

The problem of communicating the message

We do not have space here to evaluate the evidence for this astounding divine intervention. I have done so recently in my book *Jesus for Sceptics*. Whatever we make of it, there can be no doubt that the death and resurrection of Jesus formed such a powerful spring surging up from the desert of Judaean religion and politics that two thousand years later it can claim the allegiance of a third of the human race! In the thirties of the first century eleven men and a group of faithful women became utterly persuaded that God had indeed broken in to bring humanity salvation in Jesus Christ. So they set out with the momentous goal of bringing this message to the world. As far as history relates, the cost for almost all of them was martyrdom. What had inspired them? Why were they so excited, so resolute and so passionately unconcerned for their own safety?

That is a very good question. After all, the cards were stacked against them. They were so few, and they had had no training in spreading their gospel. They had no finances, no organisation behind them. And their message would seem almost incredible to their fellow Jews. For one thing, not a single one of them was an authorised rabbi. They were stigmatised as unlearned and ignorant. For another, what they had to say was highly offensive. They proclaimed that the essence of Judaism, the attempt to reach fellowship with God by temple worship and keeping the law, was impossible. They asserted that Jesus, condemned to death by their country's leadership, was in fact the long-awaited 'Messiah', or rescuer of the people, to whom the prophets had borne witness. This seemed utterly incredible. Not only had he manifestly failed to deliver his people, he had died a shameful and very public death. What is more, he had died on a cross. This was very significant to Jews. Did not Deuteronomy declare that anyone exposed on a stake rested under the curse of God (Deuteronomy 21:23)? And how could the Messiah be accursed? Clearly the claim of these first believers must have seemed ridiculous in Jewish eyes.

It was no easier to persuade Gentiles, as the first evangelists soon began to extend the message beyond the borders of Judaism: this was a further affront to the Jews who regarded Gentiles as unclean. The Greek world had long rejoiced in one of the most sophisticated of cultures. The great philosopher Plato had maintained that there is an ultimate world of forms to which the changing world of appearances points. Truth resides in these universals, not in a particular event or person, and certainly not such a squalid one as a crucified carpenter. Moreover, the Greek world worshipped a multitude of gods, even if they did not believe in them very much. So they were most unwilling to agree that a crucified peasant from a despised race could possibly be the only way to the only God!

It is apparent that these first disciples of Jesus faced an enormous task in trying to get others to believe their message, and to credit their claim that, in Jesus, God Almighty had come to their aid. We read that they themselves had fled to their homes in terror when Jesus was arrested, tried and executed. However, we find that, to their utter amazement, they were quite unable to deny the reality of the resurrection. Though the Bible records very occasional resuscitations, Jesus alone had come back from the grave to a new and lasting dimension of life. He had appeared to Peter, to all the disciples, including a pronounced sceptic like Thomas, to five hundred of his erstwhile followers at once, to Saul of Tarsus, who was a passionate enemy

21

of the new Jesus movement, and to James, the brother of Jesus. He had thought Jesus crazy during his ministry but was persuaded by an encounter with him after his resurrection, and later became the leader of the Jewish church in Jerusalem. So those first disciples were convinced. But even so they apparently said nothing. They barricaded themselves into an upstairs room for fear that the Jewish leaders would kill them as they had killed Jesus.

Pentecost: the coming of the Spirit

But one particular day changed all that. It was the Jewish Feast of Pentecost, which took place fifty days after Passover, that is to say just seven weeks since Jesus had died. He had told his followers to wait in Jerusalem for a while, and had promised that God's Holy Spirit would come upon them with power. At Pentecost that is just what happened. They received a new power, and it was life-changing.

They had long recognised God over their nation. They had slowly come to accept that God had come alongside them in Jesus. Now they were staggered to discover that God could live within them through his Spirit. For the Holy Spirit was God, no less. He had been given to the prophets, to some of the kings and occasionally to other individuals in Old Testament times. But the prophets Jeremiah and Ezekiel had predicted that the day would come when God's Spirit would be freely available to indwell his faithful people. On that day of Pentecost the disciples of Jesus realised that this had come true. Amazed and delighted, they ran into the streets, full of joy, and praising God with the new gift of tongues which had accompanied their reception of the Spirit. All fear had gone. They were so deliriously happy that people charged them with being drunk, which they easily parried by pointing out that it was too early in the day for the pubs to be open!

There was considerable symbolism attached to the initial gift of the Spirit on this particular day. Pentecost was the time to celebrate the harvest, and the first harvest of believers was gathered in, three thousand of them, on that one day. The rabbis taught that Pentecost also symbolised the giving of the law to the nations of the earth, and on this Pentecost the gospel reached representatives of all the major nations of the day who had come to Jerusalem to celebrate the feast. They came from Rome, the very heart of the empire, as well as Parthia, which lay beyond it, from Cappadocia on the Turkish steppes, and from Libya and Crete. There were Arabs and men from the Black Sea in the north and Egypt in the south. The universality of the offer of the gospel could hardly be expressed more vividly than by this amazing variety of cultures responding to God's intervention in human affairs on the first Pentecost. God had clearly broken in!

23

The impact of the first Christians

Pentecost transformed this little company of Jewish believers in the Messiahship of Jesus into a passionate new movement which soon made an impact entirely disproportionate to their numbers. They were fearless, compassionate and full of joy. They seem to have acquired new spiritual gifts, among them the 'gift of tongues'.

This gift of tongues has evoked much discussion. Some think it was the miraculous ability to speak in many languages to reach the great variety of language groups present. This is unlikely, both because all those present could speak Greek and also because it is only Peter who is recorded as giving any sort of address. In common with other uses of the phrase in the New Testament, 'tongues' almost certainly refers here to glossolalia, ecstatic prayer and praise in obscure utterances, coming from one's very heart, and was one of the special gifts of Pentecost. As we shall see throughout this book, it has not been withdrawn and frequently marks revivals of God's work. At Pentecost it seems to have had a special significance, reversing the curse of Babel and marking the unity and universality of the new movement. It was one of the signal indications of the renewing presence of God. There were others. The Acts of the Apostles tells us of a gift of healing that was sometimes accorded to some Christians. It tells of the ability to drive out dark demonic forces which were afflicting human lives. It tells us that God sometimes guides his people through visions. It tells of the astonishing unity, love and generosity that marked the infant church. It tells of the superhuman courage and bravery with which the messengers of the gospel faced every kind of peril and opposition in their passion to bring news of this 'salvation' or wholeness, for which so many were longing. All these were marks of the new life.

Inscriptions show how deep and how widespread this hunger for *soteria*, salvation, was in the Graeco-Roman world of the first century. Augustus had brought peace after a century of civil war. In the East the emperor was given titles such as *soter*, 'saviour', and *divi filius*, 'son of god'. An inscription from Philae on the Nile celebrates Augustus as 'liberator, heavenly saviour'. His inscriptions and coinage proclaimed him 'saviour of the world'. But, wonderful as his achievement had been in uniting the Roman world, at a deeper level his salvation was not enough. As Epictetus observed, 'Caesar can give peace from war, but he cannot give peace from sorrow.' And it was to this deep inner hunger for peace, for rescue from evil habits, from the fear of death and from merciless Fate, that the Christian proclamation was addressed, and made such powerful progress.

The message of these first Christians is brought clearly before us in the speeches recorded in Acts. The ancient promises to Israel had been fulfilled. God had sent his Son to be the Saviour of the world. His amazing resurrection underscored the truth of this claim. The Holy Spirit of Jesus was now active among his followers, with 'signs and wonders', as the apostles called on men and women of every race to repent of sinful rebellion against God and put their trust in Jesus, the true Saviour and Emperor of the world. Indeed, this Jesus would one day return to demonstrate his sovereignty and judge the living and the dead.

Such was the message of these intrepid pioneers as they set out on an apparently impossible mission. They wanted everyone to know about the most important thing that had ever happened, the resurrection of the Son of God from the dead. They wanted to show Jews that Jesus was the fulfilment of all God had been doing with them in the past, and to show Greeks that Jesus was the fulfilment of their quest for lasting truth, beauty and goodness.

The Acts of the Apostles is the only account we have of the first thirty years of this Christian movement. It traces its source in Jerusalem and culminates in Rome, the centre of the world. It tells of its utterly astonishing effectiveness — even bringing many of the priests in Judaism to Christ, along with the backward country people of Lystra and some of the sophisticated intellectuals at Athens. Within ten years of the death of Jesus the gospel about him had reached Alexandria and Antioch, the greatest cities in Africa and Asia respectively. Almost certainly it had reached Rome by that time: it was so notorious a movement in the capital city of the world that Christians could (wrongly!) be made scapegoats by the Emperor Nero for the Great Fire in Rome of AD 64. The message spread rapidly through the major cities of the empire, and were it not for the persecuting tendencies of Domitian there could possibly have been a Christian emperor by the end of the first century. As it was, the movement had to wait for another 230 years for that; but already it had won a multiplicity of races and cultures within the empire, already it had made inroads into the aristocracy and among the intellectuals, already it had changed the lives of countless ordinary men and women, particularly slaves. God had broken in, and in a very big way.

Opposition

Despite their incredible success, it is impossible to exaggerate the difficulties under which these early missionaries laboured. Some of it came from their neighbours. It was not just that the Christian message was unacceptable: so was their community and way of life. They said they loved their brothers and sisters — this sounded obscene even to a sex-mad Roman society. They also spoke of feeding on Christ in the Holy Communion. This sounded even worse — it was cannibalism. No wonder Christians were hated.

But they also had the imperial authorities to contend with. The Romans were very liberal in their religious policy. As they moved out in conquest over practically the whole known world they discovered in their subject peoples a multitude of gods they had never heard of. So they handled this problem in one of two ways. Either they identified the local god with one in their own extensive pantheon, or else they simply added him (or her) to that pantheon. But they did insist, in order to obtain some coherence in the empire, that subject nations should swear allegiance to Rome and Augustus, or, in the East, where men had for ages been accustomed to worship their rulers, they required obeisance to the emperor as divine. This imperial cult acted like glue in the empire. That is why Rome drew the line when any people refused allegiance to Rome and declined the requirement to burn incense before the emperor's statue once a year and say, 'Caesar is lord.' The Christians refused to do this. They were convinced that Jesus was Lord of the whole world and they would not give that title to Caesar. Consequently, they were regarded with great suspicion by the authorities. They must have seemed like a sinister secret society, about as popular with the authorities as communist cells once were in New York.

Sometimes the Christians got away with refusing to swear allegiance to Rome. At other times the suspicion and dislike this caused broke out in active persecution. The first systematic persecution we know of was under Nero in AD 64 when Christians were quite falsely accused of burning down Rome and were ruthlessly tormented and slaughtered. They were clothed in the skins of animals and attacked by wild beasts. They were covered with pitch and set alight to illuminate Nero's gardens at night. This fiendish torture disgusted even Roman writers like Tacitus, who realised that the Christians were guilty of nothing of the kind (*Annals* 15.44). There is no reliable evidence that this persecution spread beyond Rome, but after Nero's action, any provincial governor who wished to prosecute Christians was free to do so, because Roman law operated on precedent. Domitian persecuted leading Christians in the nineties, but on the whole the Christians managed to survive for long enough to spread their message of salvation very widely.

There were plenty of hungry hearts to welcome that message. Thus the gospel grew exponentially in the first fifty years after the death of Jesus. In about AD 110 Pliny the Younger, a distinguished man of letters, was appointed proconsul of Bithynia. He had not previously come across Christians, but he found to his amazement that there were lots of them in his province. So many, in fact, that temples were closing for lack of custom and sacrificial animals for the worship of the gods were hardly needed any more. He wrote to the Emperor Trajan to ask how to handle this problem. Trajan's reply was balanced. Christians should not be sought out. Action should not be taken if based on anonymous information. But if the Christians twice refused to worship the gods of Rome and the emperor, then they were clearly obstinate and should be executed (Pliny, *Letters* 10.96 and 97).

The spread of the gospel

Such were the challenges facing the first Christians. Their message was unacceptable in both Jewish and Greek circles, and their cohesive, antisocial and suspicious lifestyle seemed strange, to put it mildly, to the populace at large, and dangerous to the authorities, who were very nervous about unauthorised meetings. And yet the gospel spread everywhere it went. It filled the void that the decline of traditional Roman religion had left. It met the ancient world's hunger for close fellowship. Its message of resurrection gave a new joy in daily life and a new hope of immortality. Its offer of the Holy Spirit enabled people to improve their lifestyle. The sense of discovery displayed by these early Christians was infectious. They had discovered the famous 'philosopher's stone' which turned everything to gold. The way Christians endured persecution and torture won them the admiration of the crowd. The Stoics knew all about enduring suffering, but nothing about doing so with joy, in the assurance that their sufferings were not in vain. The message of forgiveness of sins must have been medicine to many a guilty conscience. The promise of Christ's presence with the believer must have comforted many a grieving heart. And the sheer confidence of the missionaries, sure

that God was real and had come to their aid in the
person of a recent historical figure, Jesus of Nazareth,
and sure that this Jesus, risen from the dead, was the
supreme world ruler, must have been extraordinarily
impressive. So was the unique way men and women,
slaves and free people, Jews and Greeks, mingled as
equals in worship. There was nothing like it in the
ancient world. That is why the Christians were soon
called the 'third race', being neither Jews nor Greeks,
but something different!

This, then, was the first great outpouring of the Holy
Spirit that launched the Christian Church. We shall
look at several others in this book, but they all derive
from this one source. Had Jesus not come and died and
risen, had his Spirit not been poured out on believers at
that first Pentecost, there would have been no later
revivals, no renewals of this pristine faith.

Why did God intervene at that particular time in history?

It may be vain to speculate, but it is interesting to ask
ourselves why God should have chosen this, of all times,
to come as a man to humanity. Three possible reasons
spring to mind.

First, there was now the Roman peace, the famous
pax Romana. This was immensely significant after the
internal wars that had for nearly a century

devastated the final years of the Republic, as opposing Roman generals fought for supremacy. Since Augustus' accession the world was, for the first time ever, under one rule, that of Rome. This peace was cemented by a network of roads which made extensive travel possible. Pirates were put down, Roman armies guarded the frontiers, brigands were suppressed. This meant that communications were comparatively easy, and this contributed enormously to the spread of the gospel.

Second, there was the Greek language. Rome had conquered Greece more than a century before, but had itself been captivated by the Greek language. This, even more than Latin, became the lingua franca of the ancient world, much as English is today. The sensitivity and flexibility of the language made it possible, if need be, to express complicated theological concepts with precision. And this prevalence of Greek meant that there was one language widely understood all over the empire, in which the missionaries could commend their message.

Roman peace, Greek language and, third, Jewish religion. The Jews, experts in trade and finance, had spread widely in the major cities of the empire. They were not loved, but they were reluctantly admired. Their monotheism seemed to make sense, particularly because Greek philosophy following Plato had come to recognise one god, and partly because there was now a sole ruler of the empire who claimed to be in some sense divine. Their worship, with its sung psalms and ancient writings full of wisdom, were a real attraction to Romans whose public religious observances usually consisted in reading omens based on examination of an animal's entrails. At no time, before or since, has the world been broadly under one ruler, with one language and recognition of one God. It is perhaps not surprising that God's great initiative came at this unique time in human history.

So despite the acute difficulties which beset the early Christians, these were three real advantages which favoured the spread of the faith about which they were so passionate. Christians made good use of them.

The human elements in the great outpouring

But if we grant that it was divine initiative that brought about this amazing launch of what was to become the biggest religion in the world, what were the human conditions? We cannot force God's hand for a new Pentecost, but we can look at the human conditions that facilitated the original one.

Hunger for God to act

First there was a real hunger for the Lord to come in power and act. The Jews saw it primarily as rescue from the Romans, but some of their more sensitive writers realised that something deeper was needed, a rescue from human self-centredness and sinfulness. We can see this longing in some of the inter-testamental writings such as the Psalms of Solomon, written some fifty years or so before Christ. In particular the seventeenth psalm looks forward to the Messiah. 'God will make him to be mighty by means of his Holy Spirit.' 'He himself will be pure of sin', though 'all others are sinful'. 'He shall reprove sinners for the thoughts of their hearts. He shall be a righteous king and will bless the people with wisdom and gladness. His words will be more refined than gold.' And there is a heartfelt cry to God. 'Raise up the king, the son of David.' In the New Testament itself we are introduced to two of these faithful Israelites, waiting and trusting that God would intervene: Zechariah, a priest, and Anna, an aged prophetess. Like many others they were 'looking for the redemption of Jerusalem'. That hunger for God, that dedication to him — Anna never left the temple but worshipped there with prayer and fasting night and day — was clearly one of the human conditions which facilitated God's intervention.

Humility in the first disciples

A second was the simplicity and humility of many of the first disciples. We might have expected God to reveal himself to kings, the chief priests or the emperor. But no. At the incarnation God showed his hand to poor shepherds. The followers whom Jesus selected and called were tradesmen and fishermen. They were not tempted to claim credit for themselves in the spread of the movement, but acknowledged that this was due to the Holy Spirit and were glad to glorify God for it. Humility is, sadly, not always a marked characteristic among Christians, but it is a priceless quality in God's eyes. It means he can afford to work powerfully through his servants without the danger of their becoming proud.

Enthusiasm

Another quality which stands out in these first witnesses of the resurrection is their bold enthusiasm. Unlike many of today's church members, they were full of enthusiasm. They knew themselves to be recipients of God's mercy and forgiveness. They were thrilled that not only were they brought into his family, they were given a job to do — to bear witness to the Saviour who had 'called them out of darkness into his marvellous light'.

I was driven to appreciate that enthusiasm and wholeheartedness recently when visiting Cappadocia, the great inland plateau of Turkey, three thousand feet high. It is approached from the sea via the towering Taurus range of mountains. This was the path trodden by Paul and Barnabas in their first missionary journey. More precipitous and unforgiving land it would be hard to imagine. But such was their single-minded passion to spread the good news of Christ in the interior, in towns like Pisidian Antioch, Lystra and Derbe, that we do not even get a mention in Acts of the hardships their journey entailed.

Courage

This leads naturally into another outstanding characteristic of the first believers, sheer dogged courage. They had the leaders of their nation against them, forbidding them to speak in the name of Jesus. They took no notice. They were whipped and imprisoned by the Romans, but they could still be found singing hymns to God at midnight! They were scorned, reviled, but they continued to persevere with their news of salvation. 'Many of your writers exhort to courageous bearing of pain and death,' wrote Tertullian, a second-century Christian lawyer, 'and yet their words do not find so many disciples as Christians do, teachers not by words but by their deeds.' He concluded, 'The oftener we are mowed down by you, the more in number we grow. The blood of the martyrs is seed.' That man knew what he was talking about, from much personal experience. Courage was one of the outstanding marks of the early church.

Prayer

As we shall see in the chapters that follow, earnest prayer has figured largely in all the great revivals. The first was no exception. The pages of the Acts of the Apostles are full of it. The disciples were in prayer for days before their great experience of the Spirit at Pentecost. The new converts joined them in their prayers, as well as absorbing their teaching. The apostles went regularly to the temple to pray. When the first arrests came, and Peter and John were released with a caution against ever preaching again, the first thing they did was to go to pray with their friends. We read that as a result they were all filled afresh with the Holy Spirit and went out to preach the Word of God with boldness. And so it continued. The apostles refused to get distracted even by something as important as social work (though they provided for it) but determined to 'give themselves to prayer and the ministry of the word'. Was Peter, their leader, in prison? The Christians gave themselves to fervent prayer. Fasting and prayer preceded the first missionary journey. It marked Paul's farewell to the elders at Ephesus after three years of working with them. Paul was praying in the temple when he was arrested in Jerusalem and held prisoner for two years before being able to appeal his case to the emperor. Prayer was the lifeblood of the early church. It expressed their utter dependence on God alone for the success of the work. It was his work, not theirs.

Dependence on the power of the Spirit

But the greatest of all elements in this first great surge of gospel presentation was the dependence of the disciples on the presence and power of the Holy Spirit. Before being endowed with the Spirit they were powerless. After he came upon them they were fearless. Before he came they were tongue-tied and stayed shut up in an upstairs room. After he came they are found full of joy and conviction, proclaiming their message everywhere — in homes, in the open air and in prison. The sheer power of their proclamation was notable. It was not merely the conviction with which they spoke, though this too was recognised by the pagans; but St Paul uses an interesting word, *plerophoria*, which suggests that the preachers were so full of God's Holy Spirit, so persuaded of the truth and relevance of their message that it simply overflowed from them and people received it, as 1 Thessalonians 1:5 has it, 'not simply with words but also with power, with the Holy Spirit and deep conviction (*plerophoria*)'. That was itself impressive in a society bored with the endless chatter of somewhat degenerate philosophers who were keen on their fees but seemed to have little conviction about the truth or relevance of their various opinions.

Healing and exorcism

There was, however, another dimension to this power of the Spirit. It involved healing and exorcism, and this was a fact of great importance in the spread of the gospel in a world which had totally inadequate medical services and was oppressed by belief in demonic forces.

38

The great German historian Adolf von Harnack summarises the situation well.

The whole world and its enveloping atmosphere was filled with devils: not merely idolatry but every phase and form of life was ruled by them. They sat on thrones, they hovered round cradles. The earth seemed literally a hell, though it was, and continued to be, a creation of God. To encounter this hell and all its devils the Christians had command of weapons which were invincible.

This assurance of victory was indeed the impression the Christians gave. The Gospels show beyond doubt that Jesus shared this common belief in Satan and his demons. Some recent scholars like G. B. Caird take this fact as decisive for Christian belief. Others, like Trevor Ling, reckon that we are not bound by beliefs which Jesus inevitably shared in common with people of a very different age. But all agree that Jesus did believe in these forces of evil, and that he sent out his apostles not only to preach but to heal and cast out demons. According to Luke's account, they came back to Jesus after a short mission trip, radiant with the joy of finding that these demonic forces became subject to them through his name. This continued not only in the days of the apostles, but is widely attested in the second and third centuries and beyond. Christians went out into the world as exorcists and healers as well as preachers. Acts is full of 'signs and wonders', the exorcisms and healings which backed up the Christian claim that Jesus had conquered the demonic forces on the cross and had come to bring salvation to the whole person. Peter and John did not merely proclaim good news to the cripple at the temple gate: in the name of Jesus, they healed him and enabled him to walk. Acts tells us that Paul did not merely preach at Ephesus but 'God did extraordinary miracles through Paul' (Acts 19:11), including an outstanding exorcism which led to many becoming believers and confessing their occult practices. For they collected their expensive magic books and burnt them publicly. 'In this way the word of the Lord spread widely and grew in power' (v. 20). The continuation of this powerful healing and exorcising work of Jesus can be traced through the Epistles and continued long after the apostolic age. The apologists, who gave a robust defence of Christianity in the next two centuries, refer to it again and again. Justin, for example, in the mid-second century, can issue this challenge:

And now you may learn from what goes on under your own eyes. Many of our Christians have in the name of Jesus Christ exorcised numberless demoniacs throughout the world and in your city. When all other exorcists and specialists in incantations and drugs have failed, they have healed them and still do heal, rendering the demons impotent and driving them out.

The power of the name of Jesus was more effective than any charm, and Christians were careful to distinguish it from magic. Irenaeus, the great second-century intellectual and missionary bishop, writes this about the healing and exorcism practised by the Christian Church.

Nor does she perform anything by means of angelic invocations, or by incantations or by any other wicked or curious art; but by directing her prayers to the Lord in a pure, sincere and straight-forward spirit, and calling on the name of our Lord Jesus.

In contrast to partial or temporary cures effected by the Gnostics and pagan magicians, Irenaeus insists that the cures effected by this reliance on the name of Jesus are both permanent and complete.

This all seems very strange to modern Western eyes, but we need to take account of it for two reasons. One is that it formed a major part in the evangelisation of the Roman empire in the first four hundred years, as is convincingly demonstrated by Ramsay MacMullen, Professor of Classics and History at Yale. His book *Christianizing the Roman Empire* AD *100–400* maintains that the biggest single factors in the expansion of the Church during this period were the healings and exorcisms. The other reason is that many of these phenomena associated with the first age of the coming of the Spirit, such as healings, tongues and exorcisms, have marked some, though not all, of the subsequent revivals of the Church. They are commonplace in the Chinese revival today, as we shall see in a later chapter. So if we are sceptical, it might be wise to suspend judgement. But

what is beyond doubt is that these first Christians attributed their success primarily to the power of the Holy
Spirit which attended their preaching and inspired
their lifestyle.

3

River of new life
The Reformation

Of course, there were many occasions when God broke in during the centuries following Pentecost and the birth of the Church, but in this chapter I have chosen to focus on one of the best known and also one of the most significant for Britain — although its ripples extended worldwide: the Reformation. It was not, of course, the beginning of the church in Britain — far from it. But it was a fountain of fresh water in a superstitious but spiritually barren age. If we are to understand its impact on Britain, we first need to trace in outline a little of the history of Christianity in the British Isles.

Early British Christianity

The Christian faith came to these islands sometime in the middle of the first century AD, perhaps through travelling merchants from Gaul, or perhaps it arrived with some of the soldiers in the Roman invasion of AD

43. Nobody knows. At all events Tertullian, writing around the year 200, speaks of 'places of the Britons not reached by the Romans, but subject to Christ' and adds that 'Christ's name reigns there.' Certainly the gospel was flourishing in many parts of the country well before AD 314 when three British bishops attended the Synod of Arles.

During the next three centuries the Roman forces were progressively withdrawn, and the British or Celtic church grew and had an enormous impact in the land, led by such great men as David, Patrick, Ninian, Aidan and Columba. Theirs was indigenous British Christianity. But it took a heavy battering from the onslaught of Vikings and Saxons from the continent.

Early Roman Christianity

In the sixth century an event took place which greatly changed the flavour of Christianity in Britain, bringing the island, now free of Roman military occupation, under the spiritual influence of Rome. Pope Gregory had noticed a group of handsome Saxon boys who had been brought to Rome as slaves. Told that they were Angles, he famously observed, 'Not Angles, but angels', and in 597 he sent a missionary priest, Augustine, and a group of monks to the country to re-evangelise it. Augustine was not enthusiastic! But in due course he and some monks landed in England and were able to lead the King of Kent to Christian faith. They also made some spiritual inroads into the heathen Saxons who had driven the British church into the West — particularly Wales and Cornwall. The Pope had made Augustine a bishop and had given him authority over all the English bishops — who were none too eager to accept ecclesiastical domination by Rome. So there was a very important synod at Whitby in 664, where the differing Roman and British expressions of Christianity were thrashed out. After much discussion on such things as the date of Easter and the tonsure of monks, it was eventually agreed that Christ had given the keys of the kingdom of heaven to Peter, and that therefore, as the Bishop of Rome claimed to be Peter's successor, Roman influence should prevail throughout the church in England. And so it did until the Reformation.

What was the English Reformation?

That is not as easy a question to answer as we might like it to be. It is rather complex. Was it political, a battleground between the King of England, the Holy Roman Emperor and the Pope? Was it a movement born in Germany through the actions and teaching of Martin Luther? Was it an outbreak of greed and iconoclasm, as the monasteries were dissolved, their revenues appropriated and religious images smashed? Was it the result of an over-sexed king tiring of an ageing wife and lusting for the raven locks and flashing eyes of Anne Boleyn? Or was it, perhaps, when allowance has been made for all these contributory factors, primarily a profoundly religious movement, one of the deepest rivers that have ever flowed in Christendom?

Was the English Reformation primarily political?

Some more historical background will help us here. Back in 1212 the Pope, for reasons that need not detain us, had pronounced that King John was deposed from his throne. In panic John made the most shameful submission. He grovelled before the papal legate and surrendered his kingdom to the Pope. The Bishop of Rome was now the supreme head of England, and if John received his kingdom back, as he did, it was only as a vassal of the Pope — and with the debt of a hefty annual contribution to the Vatican coffers. That situation continued. The monasteries throughout the country were like papal outposts, subject to the Pope, not to English bishops. Something like a third of the land was in the hands of the monasteries, and all this was very irksome to successive English kings. Henry VIII was determined to assert himself and bring England totally under the control of crown and Parliament, with foreign papal power excluded. Tribute should not be paid to foreign powers nor lawsuits determined by them. This was no novelty on his part. Since the Councils of Constance and Basel a century before, many in northern Europe agreed that the Pope was merely the administrative servant of the Church, and by 1534 the position was accepted by the Convocations of the Church that 'the Bishop of Rome hath not by Scripture any greater authority in England than any other foreign bishop'. Henry set out to act on this. It was a political, not a spiritual move.

Was the English Reformation due to Luther?

When in 1517 Martin Luther, monk, theology professor and iconic figure of continental Protestantism, attacked the sale of indulgences, he was heading for trouble. Indulgences were money paid to the church to secure the release of souls from purgatory. In other words, you could buy God's pardon for your sins by paying money. This scandalous practice brought inestimable wealth into the church, which was (understandably!) unwilling to let it go. Not surprising, then, that in 1520 Luther was excommunicated by the Pope and the next year outlawed by the Holy Roman Emperor. We cannot follow Luther's fascinating life and impact here, but three of his key convictions led to the break with Rome and the formation of the Lutheran Church.

First, he maintained that salvation is a *free gift of God* and cannot be purchased by either money or good works.

Second, *the Bible*, and not the church or the papacy, *is the only source of divinely revealed knowledge.*

And third, *all baptised believers form a 'holy priesthood'* and are not to be held hostage by clergy.

To be sure, all this was a great encouragement to people with reformist tendencies in England, but it did not itself produce them. As early as 1511 the king's secretary had written deploring the price of faggots because so many heretics were being burnt daily. These heretics were the followers of Wycliffe, to whom we shall turn in a moment.

Was the Reformation a grab for the monasteries?

If neither politics nor Luther can adequately explain it, was this what the English Reformation was all about? The answer must be no. The monasteries were no longer, on the whole, the centres of vital religious life they had been in the early Middle Ages. They did provide hospitality for travellers and offered some practical help for the poor, but they tended to be greedy for money and many of them were marred by gross immorality. Moreover, they were not subject to the law of the land but only accountable to the church. They had largely degenerated into half-secularised clubs for common and comfortable living. This situation proved intolerable to the king. The smaller monasteries were suppressed by an Act in 1536, but Henry had no intention of dissolving all monasteries, and actually founded two new ones the following year. To our surprise, most monasteries were not ruthlessly ravaged by the state under Henry VIII but voluntarily dissolved themselves between 1536 and 1540. No doubt they saw which way the wind was blowing. But none of the abbots in the House of Lords protested, and hardly any monks and nuns fled overseas. They received pensions, and many appeared glad to leave. There was bloodshed only when monks refused the royal supremacy. True, there was the greed of the king, who wanted their immense wealth to finance his wars and building programmes. True, the dissolution of the monasteries at the hands of Thomas Cromwell was clinical and often violent: it was by far the most important social event in the Reformation. But it is certainly not the key to understanding what the Reformation was about.

Was the Reformation the result of Henry VIII's lust for Anne Boleyn?

Even the lust of Henry for Anne Boleyn does not provide the key for understanding the Reformation. To be sure, it was a factor. Henry confessed himself 'bewitched' by her. But he had been married for eighteen years to Catherine of Aragon, and when she produced a succession of stillbirths and only one surviving girl, (later Queen) Mary, he gave himself to serious reflection. Male heirs were vital for Tudor kings. Catherine failed to produce one. Could this be God's judgement on the marriage? Henry had married Catherine when, in youth, she had been contracted to

49

his deceased brother Arthur. Perhaps they had had intercourse, in which case Henry was forbidden in Scripture to take her as his wife. So he had resorted to a papal dispensation to get round this obstacle to his marriage, but increasingly his misgivings grew. Had he been living in sin for eighteen years? He applied to Pope Clement, a weak man, for a declaration of nullity on his marriage with Catherine. The Pope avoided giving an answer for two years (had he agreed, he would have had to admit that his papal predecessor, who sanctioned the marriage, was in the wrong) and was then taken captive by the Holy Roman Emperor and Spanish king, Charles V — who was Catherine's nephew! He could scarcely grant Henry's request under those circumstances. Henry's patience was limited, and in 1533 he swore he would not recognise appeals to any foreign judge. He divorced Catherine and immediately married Anne. He was of course excommunicated by the Pope in retaliation, but he did not care in the slightest. Nevertheless, Henry was emphatically not a Reformer. He remained a Catholic to the end of his life, but, like many European leaders, rejected the authority of the Pope. The Reformation was certainly not fuelled by Henry. He wanted a Catholicism without the Pope.

The roots of the Reformation

What, then, leads us to the heart of the Reformation in England? Why has it become such a deep and satisfying spiritual 'well' for so many millions?

John Wycliffe

The answer, I believe, begins with John Wycliffe, an Oxford scholar who lived from 1320 to 1384, long before the Reformation. He was Master of Balliol College, Oxford, and the leading philosopher and theologian of his day, reputedly never worsted in debate. What is more, he was idolised by the students. Perhaps his greatest achievement was the translation of the Bible from Latin (which ordinary people could not understand) into English. Only the New Testament was completed by his death in 1384, but his colleagues translated the Old Testament, and the Bible in English was then avidly sought after, despite being strictly forbidden by church authorities. More than 150 manuscripts of his New Testament survive, which shows how widely they circulated.

As Wycliffe's studies of the Bible intensified over the middle years of his life, he became more and more overt in his criticisms of the errors in the church of his day. Thus, he argues that clergy ought to be poor, like Christ, that monasteries should be dissolved because 'monks with their great bellies and their red fat cheeks' squander the nation's wealth: the true Christian life is lived out in the world, not in the cloister. Christ is the head of the Church, not any Pope, and if there must be some visible head there is no reason why it should be the Bishop of Rome, but rather someone exemplary for holiness and humility. Scripture is the supreme standard for Christian faith and lifestyle, and the norm by which all church tradition and law should be tested. Wycliffe attacked the doctrine of transubstantiation as absurd and blasphemous. This was the view, central to the Roman Catholics, that through the act of consecration by the priest the bread and wine at Communion are miraculously transformed into the body and blood of Christ. He maintained that to worship the Host (consecrated bread) as though it was God is nothing short of idolatry.

Though he still believed in purgatory and venerated the Virgin Mary, it is not surprising that he earned for himself the name of 'the Morning Star of the Reformation' — although it would be another 150 years before that dawn turned into full sunlight.

Wycliffe's Lollards

Needless to say, all this provoked massive opposition from the clergy, and one of Wycliffe's most important achievements was the commissioning and sending out of 'poor preachers', laymen who spread his message far and wide. Called Lollards, they slowly impregnated

English society right up to the main flowering of the Reformation in the 1500s. The clergy were thoroughly alarmed, and in 1401 an Act was placed on the statute book sanctioning the public burning of heretics, as the Lollards were called. We have records of large numbers of such burnings throughout the fifteenth century, and of the incredible courage and steadfastness of the mainly common people who suffered this dreadful penalty. For example, in 1410 a West Country Lollard, John Badby, was condemned to burn at Smithfield because he would not swerve from his conviction that Christ, sitting at supper, could not give his disciples his living body to eat.

Great efforts were made to get Badby to recant. Henry, Prince of Wales and soon to become king, was among the crowd that came to witness the execution. He intervened personally, offered Badby life and money if only he would recant. That must have been a memorable sight. The hope and pride of English aristocracy had come in person to entreat a poor tailor to choose life, but he had come in vain. The pyre was lit, but the man's contortions as the flames licked at him were mistaken for a sign of submission. So Henry ordered the faggots removed, and renewed his offers and entreaties, but again to no effect. So the faggots were lit a second time, and in anguish — but in triumph — Badby went to meet his Lord. Henry V could beat the French at Agincourt, but there was something here beyond his understanding, a spiritual power and courage that became the glory of the Reformation.

All attempts to put the Lollards down failed, and in scores of villages little groups of these Christians gathered in secret to study the Scriptures and encourage one another to holy living. They would be visited by wandering preachers, men with a price on their heads, maintaining their protest against corruption in the Church, and reading the well-thumbed manuscripts of Scripture which Wycliffe had translated.

Tyndale's Bible translation

The next contributory factor to the Reformation came with the scholarly Bible translator William Tyndale (1492–1536). The clergy and monks were so afraid of the power of Scripture when let loose among the population that anyone found possessing a copy of Wycliffe's Bible could be condemned to death. But when Tyndale, profiting from Caxton's recent invention of the printing press, began to issue the first printed version of the New Testament in English, the flood could no longer be stemmed. England proved too dangerous for him, and the opposition was so fierce that he went abroad and set up shop on the continent, and in the 1520s a great many of his Bibles found their way into England through the ports as contraband, just as they did into China in the twentieth century through the work of Brother Andrew and others.

Tyndale's Bible was an improvement on Wycliffe's because for the first time it was based not on a Latin translation, the Vulgate, but on the original Hebrew and Greek manuscripts translated into English, and it became the main source for the later King James version. Tyndale, when charged with heresy before the ignorant Chancellor of Gloucester, had boldly declared, 'If God spare my life, ere many years I will cause the boy that driveth the plough shall know more of the Scriptures than thou.' He lived to see the fulfilment of that prayer, but not for long. He was betrayed, arrested, strangled at the stake and his body burned in September 1536. His final words were, 'Lord, open the King of England's eyes,' and that prayer, too, was answered. Three years later, in 1538, King Henry authorised the Great Bible, ironically largely based on Tyndale's translation, to be set up in every church so that people could read it for themselves — something hitherto unheard of. It was immensely popular, and a second edition had to be produced a year later, to which Archbishop Cranmer, who was leaning more and more to the views of the continental reformers, Luther and Calvin, wrote a commendatory foreword.

The flowering of the Reformation

The Reformation could now not be stopped, hard though Henry tried to do so. But things had already gone too far. The Pope had been repudiated, Luther's reforming influence was growing apace and Tyndale's

Bible was being avidly devoured. The monasteries were the main centres of opposition to the Reformation, but as we have seen, the monasteries were closing down. The king was also strongly opposed to the forces of reform. He remained committed to the old Catholic faith, and promulgated the reactionary Six Articles, making Protestantism a crime and denial of transubstantiation punishable by death.

But in 1547 Henry died. The reformers were now in charge, as the boy-king Edward VI, himself a convinced Protestant, reigned for only a brief six years. Archbishop Cranmer abolished the countless Latin rites held in different parts of the country and published the 1549 Prayer Book to be used everywhere. It was in English, the language of the people, and was well on the way to classical Reformation teaching. It was heavily influenced by Luther, who believed that church customs should only be altered when Scripture demanded. So Cranmer, with his sure gift for writing liturgy, brought the best elements of the old rites into the new English services of Morning and Evening Prayer and Holy Communion. But most of the outward signs of the mediaeval rite, like the stone altars and clerical vestments, remained untouched.

The book satisfied nobody. The conservatives saw it as too radical, the reformers as too conservative. Three years later Cranmer, backed by the young king, brought out the 1552 Prayer Book, which was much more explicitly Protestant and owed a lot to the view of the more radical continental reformers like Calvin that Scripture must give a warrant for every action performed in liturgy. So the statues were smashed or removed from the churches, wall paintings whitewashed over, worship of the saints abolished, every trace of transubstantiation, the mediaeval doctrine of the Mass, expunged, the altar replaced by a Communion table, vestments abolished, prayers for the dead discontinued and the clergy allowed to marry.

Queen Mary's reaction

Nevertheless, this very Reformed 1552 Prayer Book never got going among the understandably puzzled churchpeople of England, because a year later Mary, a passionate Roman Catholic, came to the throne. The Prayer Book was banished, the Catholic faith restored, Protestant legislation revoked. The Latin Mass was restored, with its vestments and ceremonies. England came again under the authority of Rome. Two thousand clergy were ejected because they had married, and leading Reformers, such as Bishops Ridley and Latimer, were imprisoned and before long burnt alive at the stake for heresy. It was as the flames were taking hold in Oxford's Broad Street outside Balliol that Latimer uttered his immortal charge: 'Be of good comfort, Master Ridley, and play the man. We shall this day light such a candle by God's grace in England as I trust shall never be put out.' It never has been.

The Archbishop of Canterbury, Thomas Cranmer, temporarily escaped the flames by recanting his Protestant convictions in the face of this fierce opposition, but finally his courage returned, and he too was burnt alive in Oxford in 1556, thrusting first into the fire the hand that had signed his recantation.

And so the relentless burnings went on until the death of Mary in 1558. And England, which had not been won to the Reformed faith by the various Acts of Parliament and prayer books of the church leaders, was captivated by the sheer courage of the martyrs. Here were men who were prepared to face the most appalling agonies because of their Christian convictions. They were heirs of the Lollards and heroes of the Reformation. At last they captured the hearts of the country.

We cannot follow this fascinating story into the religious settlement under Queen Elizabeth, which has on the whole proved so durable, nor to the impact of the Puritans which did so much to deepen holy living throughout the parishes of England. It is time to summarise the main achievements of the Reformers and the truths for which they were prepared to die. What was the river from which they drank so deeply?

The achievements and convictions
of the Reformation

Achievements

Let's take the achievements first.

Much that was corrupt or mistaken in the Church was swept away. The authority which the Pope had assumed and had so grossly abused was abolished. The monastic system, some of it good but much of it greedy and immoral, had been judged and found unworthy. Three wrong beliefs which had grown up in the Middle Ages were exposed and rejected. One was the invocation of the saints as a way of ensuring God's favour, along with the system of pilgrimages and relics that had clustered around it. A second was the doctrine of purgatory with its frescoes on the church walls of the agonies of the dead, along with its chantries and Masses for the departed. Third was the doctrine of transubstantiation, with its altars and vestments, which had obscured the meaning of the Holy Communion.

But the Reformation did far more than sweep away what was false. It brought great blessings to the country. There was now an open Bible in every church, and all were encouraged to read and study it. There were services in English in every parish church which the poorest labourers could understand and share in. There was an open way into the presence of God because of Christ's death, which did not necessitate the mediation of a priest. There was the abolition of the requirement for confession before a priest, but its continued use was permitted for those who found it helpful. And there was the great truth that the Christian priesthood is shared by all believers. All have direct access to God. All are called to be God's representatives in society. The Reformation did not constitute a new church. It was the same church which had been in Britain for fifteen hundred years. But it had now received a thorough bath and suit of new clothes.

Convictions

First was *the supremacy of Holy Scripture*. The mediaeval church had not allowed laypeople to read the Bible and had strayed a very long way from the teachings of the New Testament. Once the Bible was readily available in the language of the people, it became the touchstone by which both the faith and practice of the Church were judged. This was, of course, happening on the continent as well. There was a great surge of longing in the late fifteenth and early sixteenth century for a radical reformation of the Church, and what happened in England was paralleled to a large extent in Switzerland, Germany, Sweden, Denmark and elsewhere. It was the Bible that fed this longing and directed its path.

Second was the central Reformation rediscovery of *justification through God's grace alone*, received by faith alone rather than by human good works. This transformed the religious scene. You did not need a priest, a monk or a pope to put you right with God. You did not need to get shriven and receive the Mass daily in order to sustain your Christian life. You did not need chantry chapels to have Masses sung for your soul when you died. For Christ had smashed the power of death and was waiting to welcome his followers when they died. Much that had cluttered up mediaeval religion was cleared away, and men and women could know they were put right with God because of what Christ had achieved for them once and for all on the cross, and could seek to conform their way of life to the teaching of the Scriptures. And in their corporate life, they could attend a church where the services were in English and gospel preaching and the reading of homilies, full of wholesome teaching, was required. This was an incalculable blessing.

A third deep conviction was the priesthood of all believers. Mediaeval priests had to be unmarried and they claimed control of access to God. It was they who baptised. It was they who offered Christ to churchpeople in the Mass. It was they who consigned people to hell by excommunication. All this was swept away by the reformers. They saw that the New Testament knew nothing of a category of priests mediating between the believer and God. They saw that the New Testament knew nothing of transubstantiation, let alone a special cadre of officials who could administer it. And they saw that the New Testament knew nothing of enforced

61

celibacy for Christian leaders. All Christians have direct access to God. All have the responsibility of representing him to unbelievers. All may marry if they wish. This was revolutionary indeed!

A fourth great conviction was that *the gospel was worth suffering and dying for*. The accession of Queen Mary seemed to herald the end of the Reformation, as Catholicism with its Latin Mass and its vestments was restored, and the country returned to the Pope's allegiance. But surprisingly the Reformation was not undone. Some of the Protestants had fled abroad, but most stayed and refused to compromise with the return of Roman Catholicism. If they were to be rooted out, it had to be done by force, so firm were their convictions. Persecution set in. Many were burnt alive, and the stench of burning human flesh was commonplace. Stories of how the martyrs met their end spread like wildfire around the country. Bishop Hooper died at the stake in a slow fire outside Gloucester Cathedral, with a pardon lying on a stool before his eyes which he could have claimed at any time if only he would recant. As we have seen, the Archbishop of Canterbury and two senior bishops met the same fate. Laymen were as courageous as clergy. We read of a barber, an apprentice boy, a butcher and an old Welsh fisherman laying down their lives in the flames. Some went to their deaths singing psalms until the fire consumed them. One horrible story recounts the burning of a woman who gave birth in the flames, and the baby, initially rescued, was tossed back into the fire. The courage of these heroes was indomitable. They had found in the gospel, so long obscured in the mediaeval church, a treasure more valuable than life itself. And their courageous suffering did more than anything else to turn the country to the Reformed faith.

So the greatest achievement of the Reformation was the rediscovery of a dynamic, life-changing New Testament faith, which could lead men and women to withstand the most terrible persecution like their forefathers in the first three centuries. Here was a faith to live by. Here was a faith worth dying for. And the manner of their dying inspired many others to follow them. These men and women had drunk from a river which had long flowed underground. They had experienced for themselves the cold refreshing waters of Scripture, justification through faith and personal intimacy with Christ without the need for human intermediaries. Moreover, they had seen the proof of its power in the way the martyrs died.

The Reformation's challenge for us today

In today's Church we need to recover this emphasis on biblical teaching, not least in sexual matters where church leaders all too easily follow secular opinion, even when it is manifestly opposed to the teaching of the Bible. We need to recover their emphasis on the sacrifice of Christ on the cross as the one way for sinners to get reconciled with God, rather than surrender to the pluralist propaganda which seeks to persuade us that all religions are much the same and that they all lead people to God. We need to oppose clericalism and foster lay leadership alongside ordained. We need to be willing to stand up for our faith however unpopular it may be — to go to prison if necessary, even to die for our beliefs. And we need to take on board the fact that God's timing is not necessarily our own. It took nearly two hundred years for the spiritual renewal under the Lollards to reach its fulfilment in the Elizabethan settlement. Too often we want immediate answers and are not prepared for the long haul. But true reformation is always prepared to await God's timing in faith and patience.

4

The springs erupt
The Awakening

One of the greatest spiritual awakenings ever to be seen in Britain took place in the eighteenth century under the leadership of John and Charles Wesley and George Whitefield. It was indeed a fulfilment of that early Christian song, 'Wake up, sleeper, rise from the dead, and Christ will shine on you.' The soul of England was dead, the Church fast asleep, and yet God broke in with sovereign power to transform the whole situation – all within a single generation.

Midnight: the early eighteenth century

By this point the 'river' afforded by the Reformation two centuries previously had dried up. The 'well' had been filled with rubbish, and the prospects both in society at large and in the Church looked about as bad as could be.

65

The state of society

Despite the wealth of the country under its able prime minister, Sir Robert Walpole, British society had sunk to a very low level. First, England was proverbial for drunkenness. This was as true of the nobility as it was of the ordinary people. Most business was conducted in the taverns. The squires boasted of being 'six-bottle men' — who nowadays could drink six bottles of port at a sitting? One contributing factor to this came about when the government tried to resolve a trade dispute with France by removing all tax from British spirits. You needed a licence to sell beer, but now anyone was at liberty to distil and sell gin without one. Immediately thousands of gin shops sprang up all over London. It was sold from barrows in the streets with the famous sign, 'Drunk for a penny, dead drunk for twopence, clean straw for nothing'. The whole land was sodden with drink.

Closely associated was the immorality of the age. The king, the prime minister and the Prince of Wales were all living in open adultery. Labourers even sold their wives in the cattle market, and fornication was everywhere. Theatres constantly put on indecent plays and the literature of the day was steeped in filth, from the gross obscenity of Fielding to the snide nastiness of Sterne. (This was the origin of the prejudice in evangelical circles against novels and the stage, most of which were obscene, as well as against alcohol.)

A third characteristic of life in the early eighteenth century was cruelty. Cock fighting to the death, bear baiting and the torture of animals seem to have characterised the population. There are records of bulls and dogs being dressed up with fireworks, ignited and then let loose for the amusement of the populace. But the greatest attraction was public executions. There were some 253 offences on the Statute Book for which you could be hanged. They included such small offences as stealing a loaf of bread or picking a pocket. There was no drop for hanging in those days, so the poor victims, women and children as well as men, writhed in agony at the end of the rope for half an hour or more before expiring. Sometimes friends broke through the crowd to pull on their legs and hasten their deaths. At all events, public hangings were a major entertainment for all classes of society.

But highwaymen like Dick Turpin are the best known element in the social life of the early eighteenth century. These were no altruistic and lovable rogues like the legendary Robin Hood and his men who robbed the rich to help the poor. They were ruthless and self-centred, as were the wealthy young bloods known as Mohocks who terrorised London society in the early eighteenth century. This was one of the criminal gangs derived from the days of the Restoration, and they engaged in crime for the sheer hell of it. They were reputed not to steal money, but to put old women in barrels and roll them down a hill, and to slit men's noses or cut off their hands. The forces of law and order were quite unable to restrain them, and people travelled in fear and never, willingly, at night.

The state of the Church

To what extent was the Church salt and light in a society as corrupt and demoralised as this? The answer must be 'not at all'. The Church was like the Laodicean church rebuked in the book of Revelation: 'neither hot nor cold'. Rationalism and absenteeism seem to have been its outstanding characteristics. The educated clergy hated 'enthusiasm' and believed in God as an entirely rational being. They paid little attention to Scripture and seemed to care nothing for Jesus, but encouraged an anaemic and tolerant morality. The lawyer Blackstone is reputed to have heard most of the preachers in London and claimed that none of the sermons he heard contained more Christianity than the writings of Cicero. The faith of the Reformation was completely abandoned.

Not only did the clergy not believe much, but they were rarely to be found in their parishes. They often lived comfortable, wealthy lives and farmed their lands. Rectors did not usually live in their parish. Many of them held a number of benefices, which they never visited. Instead, their curates rode out on a Sunday morning to gabble through a service and then ride on. The sexton would mount the tower on a Sunday morning, and when he saw the clergyman coming he would ring the bell to gather the congregation. Many of the churches did not even own a Bible or a prayer book and had only one service a month. There was no pastoral care, because the curate immediately after taking the service would mount his horse and go off to the next parish. The church buildings themselves often fell into disrepair, with shattered windows and broken roof, but nobody cared. The rectors enjoyed their salaries but not their work. The country was coarse, drunken and lawless, and the Church was complacent, effete and to all intents and purposes spiritually dead. The Frenchman Montesquieu on visiting England remarked, 'In England there is no religion, and the subject if mentioned in society, excites nothing but laughter.' The most intellectual cleric of the day, the able philosopher-theologian Bishop Butler, wrote, 'It has come to be taken for granted that Christianity is not so much a subject for enquiry, but that it is now at length discovered to be fictitious.'

Such was England and its church in the early eighteenth century. The land was a desert, crying out for springs of living water. That longing was answered: not from the writings of the erudite Bishop Butler, but from the fearless and unconventional ministry of two recent Oxford students, Wesley and Whitefield.

The hour before the dawn: the Holy Club

Had the Revd Samuel Wesley and his wife Susanna completed their family with fourteen children, the history of the world would have been different. But they had more children! John Wesley and subsequently his brother Charles were born into this clergy household at the outset of the eighteenth century. Their home, Epworth Rectory, was destroyed by a fire, and this made an indelible impression on 8-year-old John, who later loved to refer to himself as 'a brand plucked from the burning' (cf. Zechariah 3:2). This proved to be true of him in more ways than one.

After school he entered Oxford, where he excelled. In those days there were almost no lectures, no sport, no examinations and very little learning. The academics were for the most part lazy, gluttonous and proud. The students spent the majority of their time forming all sorts of private societies and drinking clubs. John and Charles Wesley, however, along with a couple of friends, being much more serious-minded than their colleagues, instead formed the Holy Club, where they met regularly to read the Greek New Testament. Soon they felt driven to regulate every aspect of their lives by what they saw to be the laws of God, and by 1735 there were fourteen of them, including three college tutors, one of whom was John Wesley himself. By this time he was ordained, and combined his academic work at Lincoln College with being his father's curate for a couple of years.

Needless to say, the Holy Club attracted much mockery. But they continued to meet each evening to review what they had done that day and plan for the morrow. Soon, with the bishop's permission, they started visiting in Oxford Prison, holding services and preaching, and trying to meet some of the desperate needs of these prisoners, who were kept in appalling conditions. They read the church fathers together, and longed for a return of the dynamic Christianity of the early church. But all the time their lives were like a desert. There was no spring of living water. None of them had yet entered into a personal relationship with Christ, although they bore all the marks of earnest religion.

The most famous recruit to the Holy Club was George Whitefield. He was the son of an innkeeper in Gloucester, and attended Pembroke College as a 'servitor' who sustained himself at university by waiting on some of the wealthier students. He shyly joined the others in the Holy Club and became even more excessive than they in his fasts, devotions and acts of self-denial, such as kneeling in prayer all night in the rain. He stumbled across the idea of 'new birth' in a book by a Scot, Henry Scougal, and exclaimed, 'I must be born again a new creature! Christ must be formed in me', but he still did not understand, so he intensified his religious observances.

One day he met a half-drowned woman, the wife of one of the jailbirds he visited. Desperate because she had no money to feed her children, she had tried to commit suicide, but someone had pulled her out of the Thames and, guilt-ridden, she called to George for help. He cared for her immediate physical needs and agreed to meet her and her husband in the prison that afternoon. He spoke to them about John 3:16, the most famous verse in the Bible. Suddenly the woman cried out, 'I believe, I believe. I shall not perish because I believe in him now. I am born again, I am saved.' Her husband grasped Whitefield's hand. 'I am on the brink of hell!' he exclaimed, and then, 'Oh, I see it too, I am saved! O joy, joy, joy!'

George was astonished. He had laboured for a whole year to get right with God and failed. These two seemed to have found the way in a moment.

It was not long before he found it too. He had renewed his fasting to such an extent that he fell ill and collapsed. Reading a devotional book in his room and reflecting on the crucifixion, he cried out, as Jesus had done, 'I thirst.' It was a cry of utter helplessness. He realised that he could never work his way to God, but that Christ had done all that was needed for his forgiveness. He had at last thrown himself without struggle into God's hands and experienced that new birth for which he longed. 'Joy unspeakable!' he cried. 'When the Lord turned the captivity of Zion, we were like those that dream. Then was our mouth full of laughter and our tongue with singing.'

Soon the Holy Club members left Oxford and went their separate ways. The Wesleys went as missionaries to Savannah in Georgia, and George to a curacy, before following them to America. For John Wesley America proved disastrous. His missionary work achieved nothing, and he experienced a failed love affair. He returned, depressed, to England, and wrote in his journal, 'I came here to convert the Indians, but O God, who shall convert me?' He was very struck by the deep peace which was so evident in Moravian missionaries travelling back on the same boat as himself, when they were all engulfed in a fearsome storm. They had something priceless, a peace which he knew he lacked.

It was not long after his return that he, like George, found it. He went to a little religious meeting in London's Aldersgate Street. Someone was reading from Luther's *Preface to the Epistle to the Romans*. As he listened, Wesley grasped the central truth of the gospel for himself. 'I felt my heart strangely warmed,' he wrote. 'I felt I did trust Christ, Christ alone, for salvation, and an assurance was given that he had taken away my sins, even mine.' This is rightly seen as his conversion. Although he had been very religious, learned in the Scriptures, a clergyman and a missionary, he had not before this come humbly to Christ for salvation. He had been trying to save himself. Suddenly he saw that justification before God could never be achieved by human effort but was freely provided as a result of Christ's death on the cross, a gift which he needed to receive in adoring faith. And on that day, 24 May 1738, this dedicated, intellectual but spiritually blind cleric discovered for himself that new birth which his brother Charles and George Whitefield had experienced a little earlier.

The new day: the Great Awakening

The false dawn of religious effort in the Holy Club was over. The new day of joyful trust in the finished work of Christ had dawned. And now events began to erupt at great speed.

Whitefield returned from America to be ordained priest and to gather funds for his orphanage project in Georgia. He landed in Bristol and on his first Sunday afternoon, in February 1739, went to nearby Kingswood where there were thousands of coal miners. He did what he had often done in Georgia: he stood on a little mound and started preaching to them about how they could get right with God. This created a sensation. Miners crowded to hear him, sometimes as many as 20,000 at once, for he had a fine voice and loved nothing more than preaching in the open air. It must have been so moving to see the white gutters made by tears as they ran down these men's cheeks, blackened with coal dust. Surprised by the impact of this open-air preaching but realising its importance, he saw that it must not be confined to a single city. So he set out to preach to the multitudes in the open air of London, and encouraged John Wesley to come in his place to Bristol.

Wesley was such a scrupulous churchman that he could hardly bring himself to preach anywhere but in church. However, once he did, and saw its power, he knew he had found his life's vocation.

There were so many sides to this remarkable spiritual awakening in eighteenth-century England that I am going to select just six which were very significant then and could be both a challenge and an encouragement for us today.

Open-air ministry

As we have seen, Whitefield stumbled into open-air preaching in Kingswood, and soon drew Wesley into it. They both revelled in its power. Here were men so sure of their God, so confident in his forgiveness, that they could not keep quiet, nor could they confine their preaching to Sundays only. They would often preach four or five times a day as they rode around the country. Sometimes in the early days they had to stand preaching in the street without an audience until they started singing a psalm, which drew a few children. Their mothers followed, and then some of the men, and soon there was a reasonable crowd. But before long the very names of Wesley and Whitefield drew vast crowds, often numbering several thousand. The preachers rarely ran an 'after meeting' or counted the heads of those who responded. They preached, they invited people to turn to Christ and they departed, leaving the results to God, who alone could bring about the new birth. Those who had truly been born again soon became apparent, and would often show up at the early morning prayer meeting the next day. They were then introduced to the 'class meetings' which Wesley organised, to which we shall turn below. These meetings welcomed both those who had been converted and those who were still struggling to find God and abandon their life of sin. Meanwhile the evangelists had moved on, to and fro across the country, preaching in the streets, at the market crosses and in the fields.

This was indeed a wake-up call to the eighteenth-century church.

Open-air preaching was not illegal, but it simply did not happen! The only irregularity committed by these field preachers was that they were always operating in someone else's parish. Whitefield could justify this because he had to travel throughout the country to raise funds for his orphanage in Savannah. Wesley's fellowship at Lincoln College Oxford exempted him from parish work. He wrote 'I was not limited to any particular cure, but have an indeterminate commission to preach the Word of God in any part of the Church of England.' Famously he later proclaimed that the world was his parish. Not all the clergy appreciated his position, especially when he drew great crowds in their parish!

The message of God's grace

The two great leaders in the Awakening were very different in their style of preaching, but very similar in their message. George was the natural orator, with an unusual ability to be heard at great distances and to grip the hearts of poor and rich, educated and uneducated alike. He was never more at home than when preaching in the open air, and the heart of his message was the new birth. Baptism, moral improvement, churchgoing, religious observance would not get you into the kingdom of God. Only the new birth would suffice, and that is God's sovereign work, but the human conditions are repentance from sin and trust in Christ. A distinguished lady came to hear him preach one morning. He spoke on the text, 'You must be born again.' Fascinated, she came again in the evening, and the burden of his message was the same. She caught up with him afterwards and enquired why he repeated the same message. His reply reveals his passion and his single-mindedness: 'Because, madam, you *must* be born again.'

Wesley's preaching was more precise, with short sentences and no pretention to oratory. He even read his sermons to begin with. But he too became fluent in extempore preaching. He would major on human guilt, on what Christ had done on the cross for our salvation, and the possibility of free acceptance with God as a result. Time and again we read in his journal, 'I offered them Christ', 'I proclaimed the grace of our Lord Jesus

Christ', 'I declared the free grace of God', 'I began to call sinners to repentance', 'I invited all guilty, helpless sinners'. Both preachers, despite their slightly different theological emphases, were determined not just to impart information, like most of the eighteenth-century preachers, but to preach for decision, so that the hearers did not merely hear the Word of God but felt it and responded to it.

The news that God loved them despite what they were like, the fact that Christ had died for each of them personally, and the wonder of free access to this gracious God had an immediate and profound effect on the country. The word spread like wildfire. Often people fell to the ground under conviction of sin, contorted with anguish before they came into the assurance of the new life offered them in Christ. The aim of these evangelists was as simple as it was revolutionary — to save souls.

Lay leaders

The massive response to the preaching of Wesley and Whitefield meant that they could not possibly respond to all the calls made on them, especially as Whitefield gave more than half of his time to the American colonies. So Wesley decided on the unconventional and adventurous step of commissioning lay preachers to help him in the work. Because he knew this would arouse great clerical opposition (as it did!), he armed himself with precedents from the early church and the mediaeval preaching friars.

The task of these lay leaders was to do some of the preaching. They were passionate to make Christ known, but of course they had limited learning and no recognition by the Church. Yet they travelled all over the country with the gospel. Off they went, in all weathers, with their tiny library and spare clothes all packed into their saddlebags. They slept in flea-ridden taverns, faced riots, were ducked in the local pond, put in the stocks or pelted with manure. But they saw the revival spreading inexorably across the land. Some failed, but the majority proved to be heroic soldiers of the cross.

The class meeting

The other main role played by laymen in the revival that was breaking out proved to be just as important. What was to be done with new believers? They could not be left to the tender mercies of local clergy — most of whom were absentees, anyhow. Some of them came to the 5.00 a.m. prayer meetings that Wesley held. But clearly they needed nurture. So Wesley decided on another plan which would be unconventional but not against church order. Religious societies were not unknown or forbidden. Indeed, it was at a meeting of one of these that Wesley himself had been converted. So while encouraging the converts to attend their parish church on Sundays, Wesley urged them to get together mid-week to pray, sing and help each other in the Christian life. These meetings were led by the laymen that he was training up, and they flourished. Indeed, they were the seeds from which the Methodist Church in due course developed. Wesley himself remained (in theory at least!) an Anglican until his death, but many of his converts found the 'class meetings', as they were called, so helpful and the church services so dreary that a split became inevitable. The new converts who remained in the Church of England became known as evangelicals while those who left retained the name (originally applied to the whole movement) of Methodist. At all events, the value of these small groups was inestimable. They produced accountability among members, fellowship and mutual encouragement to live a devout and disciplined Christian life. It is a tribute to Wesley's organisational gifts and the speed with which the revival took hold that he wrote the (rather rigorous) conditions for membership of these class meetings on Christmas Day 1738. Remember that he had returned from America, humiliated and as yet unconverted, as recently as February that same year!

Hymns

If Whitefield was the greatest orator of the Awakening, and John Wesley the best organiser, the great contribution of John's brother Charles was the creation of many outstanding hymns. These acted both as a wonderful means of expressing the love, enthusiasm and gratitude of the members and also as a teaching tool, a 'body of divinity'. Most church people gain their doctrine not from books or creeds but from their hymns. These converts certainly did. Charles Wesley had the gift of writing hymns full of biblical truth and musical vitality. 'O for a Thousand Tongues to Sing', 'Soldiers of Christ Arise', 'Love Divine, All Loves Excelling', 'Hail the Day that Sees Him Rise', 'Jesu, Lover of My Soul' are but a few of his great hymns, and the marvel is that they are sung with just as much passion and conviction now, two hundred and fifty years after he wrote them, as they were then. He was not alone. In fact the revival spawned many hymn writers. William Williams wrote 'Guide Me, O Thou Great Jehovah', Toplady 'Rock of Ages' and Peronnet 'All Hail the Power of Jesus' Name'. Wesley had no shortage of good material when he compiled his hymn book. Through it he determined that the poorest and most unlearned worshippers would grasp by heart the great doctrines of the faith which they were singing.

Holiness

It is important to understand that Wesley and Whitefield did not preach a free grace which exempted you from good works. They insisted that real faith produces real change of life. 'By salvation,' wrote Wesley, 'I mean not merely deliverance from hell but a present deliverance from sin, a restoration of the soul to its primitive health, a recovery of the divine nature.' And this salvation is received by faith, which is not mere assent to any number of opinions or creeds, but wholehearted trust in Christ, and the surrender of one's entire life to him. It is brought about by the action of the Holy Spirit. For it is the Holy Spirit who brings a person to repentance and commitment. It is the Holy Spirit who then enters a person's life at the new birth. And it is the Holy Spirit who nourishes that new birth into holy living. Wesley and Whitefield were both insistent upon the work of the Spirit in this transformation of human beings, and were constantly urging their converts to use the means of grace to grow in holiness. Wesley's objective, ever since his conversion, was 'to spread scriptural holiness over the land'. Whitefield's was the same. The results spoke for themselves. Lives were transformed: the drunkards became sober, the dissolute chaste, the liars truthful, the proud humble and the godless godly. The fruit of the movement was extensive and undeniable.

Rays of sunlight: their message for our day

We cannot engineer a time of spiritual awakening such as happened in this amazing eighteenth-century revival. Nor can we reproduce the social and political conditions which were so wonderfully reformed. But we can take heart from the fact that within a single generation the face of England was transformed by the gospel of God's grace. We can be encouraged to believe God can do something similar again.

Whether or not we will be privileged to see a comparable movement of God's Spirit in our day, there are certainly crucial lessons to be learnt by the modern church from this eighteenth-century revival. Here are some of them. You will be able to think of others.

We need to recognise that baptism, even ordination, does not by itself make you a Christian. To be sure, baptism is the sign, but the new birth is the thing signified. Baptism without the new birth by God's Holy Spirit did not make Wesley or Whitefield Christians, nor does it today. If we learn anything from this movement it is that you can have all the externals of religion, you can be baptised, be ordained, be a missionary, and yet remain a stranger to the gospel of God's grace and be lost eternally. We should not be embarrassed to proclaim this boldly, unpopular though it will certainly be. There are some unconverted ministers in the churches. There are some baptised unbelievers in the pews. They have never come to God in repentance and cried out for the new birth, and that accounts for much of the powerlessness of the Church.

Another important lesson to learn from the Awakening is that laypeople can be preachers of the gospel and can run effective training courses. If these are kept exclusively in clerical hands the Church will be the poorer.

The current shrinking of church membership in England is driving clergy to give greater scope to lay leadership, but I do not sense any careful training undertaken, nor initiatives like open-air ministry encouraged. It is hard for laymen to take an initiative if the vicar is against it. There is still something of a clerical stranglehold on the Church.

The Awakening drew attention to a third vital element in any renewing of God's people: the value of the small group or 'class meeting'. It is here that fellowship can be gained and accountability encouraged. The Methodist Church has largely abandoned these meetings and the Church of England has failed to adopt them strategically. This is particularly tragic in the rural areas, where anything up to a dozen parishes are combined under one clergyperson who cannot possibly exercise pastoral care among them all. We should have taken Wesley's path and trained godly laymen to run small groups, meeting in homes in every parish, with the ordained ministers seeing their role as one of encouraging and training the group leaders. They could provide springs of living water in the desert of many a rural parish. It is not too late to start. There are of course 'fellowship groups' in many places, but apart from Alpha courses and Christianity Explored they tend to lack the training, the discipline and the accountability that make for spiritual vitality.

Every renewal produces new songs for use in worship. They are the outworking of gratitude in hearts that know themselves to be redeemed. So we must not allow traditionalism to reject new hymns and choruses. But remembering that what they sing is for most people what they believe, we must be very careful not to go overboard on slushy and sentimental choruses which do not root the worshippers in the solid truths of the gospel.

Finally, the emphasis placed by leaders of the Awakening on holiness is much needed today. We have almost lost the sense of awe before God, and the determination to be conformed to the pattern of Christ in every particular which marked these great leaders. Holiness is not a notable characteristic of the twenty-first-century church. Until we hunger for it, we are unlikely to see a great renewing work of God in our own day. The rubbish must be cleared out of the wells before the populace at large will be inclined to come and drink.

5

The healing streams
The nineteenth century

Hitherto we have seen something of three divine geysers surging powerfully out of the moral and spiritual desert, first at Pentecost, then at the Reformation and, third, during the Awakening of the eighteenth century. Now, at the end of the eighteenth and the beginning of the nineteenth centuries, we see God breaking in again to broaden the scope and impact of these 'springs' of refreshing water.

The Awakening was to a large extent spearheaded by two men, Wesley and Whitefield. What I have called the 'healing streams', half a century and more later, drew on a wider circle of human agencies, but the initiative and power, as ever, lay with God.

After Wesley and Whitefield

The impact of the revival under these two men was enormous, particularly among the ordinary people of England. But most of the church leadership remained stoutly opposed to all they stood for. Drunken, lazy, absentee clergy continued. Some churches were completely neglected. Cirencester, for instance, had had no vicar since the Reformation! The living had been called a perpetual curacy and was held on licence from the bishop. But when in 1778 the curate was touched by the Awakening, the office of vicar was speedily revived and a Revd Smith appointed. He dismissed the curate, let the vicarage and continued to live in Gloucester. This illustrates both the corruption in the church leadership and their antipathy to those who, influenced by the Awakening, became known as Methodists or evangelicals. The two were identical originally, as we have seen, but gradually the term 'Methodists' was applied to those who drifted into dissent, and 'evangelicals' to those who stayed within the Church of England. It is worth remembering that this Awakening took place originally entirely in the Church of England, and its leaders were clergymen. Wesley proclaimed repeatedly that he would never leave the Church of England. Shortly before his death in 1791 he declared, 'I live and die a member of the Church of England, and none who regard my judgment or advice will ever separate from it.' But separate they did, for three main reasons.

First, because of the bitter hostility of the parish clergy and the scurrilous tracts put out against them, claiming that Wesley was expelled from Oxford for gross immorality, that he was really a Mohammedan or a Jesuit in disguise, or that he and his followers were 'furious disciples of the Antichrist, reverend scavengers, filthy poets and plagues of mankind'.

The second reason was the legal status of the preaching houses, built to accommodate the large congregations which the Awakening drew. These were not intended to be rivals of the parish churches and did not meet on Sundays, but inevitably they provoked clerical opposition. The only way Wesley could get these preaching houses licensed was by presenting them as chapels in which, under Act of Parliament, Protestant dissenters were exempted from the penalties of certain laws. This was a real, though involuntary, breach with the Church of England.

The third reason was even more decisive. Wesley was deeply distressed at the situation in North America where there was not a single bishop to ordain clergy or conduct confirmations. He begged the Bishop of London, who was technically responsible, to send one, but in vain. His studies of the New Testament and the early fathers had persuaded him that 'bishop' and 'elder or presbyter' were different names for the same office, a view which many Christians hold. So he himself consecrated a bishop for America, one Dr Coke. That action made the split with the established church inevitable.

Thus began the division between the 'enthusiasts' who remained in the Church of England and those who left. The split was a great blow to the movement, and inevitably lessened its impact on the country. A further difference lay in the itinerant nature of the Methodist preachers, who regarded the whole country as their sphere of operations, while the evangelicals tended to stay within the boundaries of their own parish. Another problem for the movement was the growing, and at times acrimonious, doctrinal division between Whitefield, who laid great stress on God's calling and election, and Wesley, who stressed humanity's free will in responding to the gospel. Moreover, because, after Wesley's death in 1791, there was no powerful personality to hold the Methodists together, divisions broke out among them and their influence waned.

Meanwhile, in the Church of England the advance of the gospel was difficult and distinctly patchy. Bishops and clergy remained very hostile to the enthusiasts who preached the grace of God, the death of Christ and his life-transforming power. They preferred formal services (conducted no more often than strictly necessary) and preached a dull and conventional morality. There was only one evangelical congregation in London, led by the gentle and scholarly William Romaine. He was not the vicar of St Dunstan's, the famous old church in Fleet Street, but had a 'lectureship' there which allowed him to preach in the afternoon. The crowds packed the church. The vicar objected. The parishioners complained their seats were occupied, and the time of his lecture was moved to 7.00 p.m. The churchwardens refused to light or warm the building, and so the preacher stood in the pulpit of a dark church holding a candle while vast numbers of people groped their way to the seats or crammed the aisles! Such was the treatment meted out to the best preacher in the city – people came from far and wide 'to see Garrick act and to hear Romaine preach'.

But the evangelicals found a doughty supporter in Lady Huntingdon, who could, as the daughter and wife of an earl, appoint her own (evangelical!) chaplains and whose home was always open for spiritual meetings, sometimes addressed by Whitefield himself. These drew the most fashionable crowds in the city. She sold her jewels in order to buy houses in other parts of the country where similar meetings could be held. But in the end, opposition to these mission services led her to abandon the Church of England and found the dissenting Countess of Huntingdon's Connexion, which still exists in a small way today. Nevertheless, her support had sustained the ministry of Whitefield for thirty invaluable years.

In other parts of the country a sprinkling of famous evangelicals held churches: men like Fletcher of Madeley in the Severn valley, Grimshaw of Haworth in the Yorkshire moors, and John Newton in Olney, a large Buckinghamshire village, inhabited 'by the half starved and ragged of the earth'. His had been a celebrated conversion from an evil life and captaincy of slave ships. He was eventually ordained and became extraordinarily influential through the pastoral letters he wrote and the hymns he composed for his mid-week prayer meeting, many of which, like 'Amazing Grace', we sing today.

But these men were exceptions, and on the whole the country was spiritually dark in the decades following the Wesleys and Whitefield. Unitarianism, belief in God but not in the distinctive truths of Christianity, was becoming the accepted creed of many educated people. Vice of every kind was on the increase. And there was a deep-seated fear that what had happened in the Reign of Terror during the French Revolution following 1789 might spill over into England. Revolution was in the air, and had recently removed the American colonies from British rule. Britain was left alone to fight Napoleon, while the king, George III, suffered recurring bouts of madness. The situation was dire. Such was the desert in which once again God created a spring of living water. It carved out several channels.

The anti-slavery channel

The most famous name in this second phase of the Awakening was William Wilberforce. A Yorkshireman born in 1759, he was small and sickly, with poor eyesight. He was educated at Hull Grammar School, but spent more time in theatres and at cards and dances than in his studies. Much the same was true of his time at Cambridge. He just managed to get a degree, but concentrated more on the social round, where his ready wit and charm made him popular. His close friend at university, William Pitt, later to become prime minister, encouraged him to stand for Parliament, and he gained a seat in 1780 while still an undergraduate. Here his oratory, his singing and his gambling made him quite a celebrity. James Boswell says of his speaking, 'I saw what seemed a mere shrimp climb the table, but as I listened he grew and grew until the shrimp became a whale.'

Although he had been somewhat intrigued by evangelicals in early life, there was nothing to show for it until his spiritual awakening while on a tour of Europe in 1784. His journals show how this conversion changed his inner life. He rose early and spent three hours with the Bible and in prayer each morning. He was immensely disciplined in time, money and self-examination. He lived out his Christianity through his politics, hard though it was because of the contempt in which those who took their faith seriously were held by their parliamentary colleagues.

Soon he was appalled to discover, from the researches of a friend, the terrible conditions in which slaves were transported from Africa to America, and the ghastly cruelties inflicted on them there. The slave trade was enormously profitable and popular among European merchants. Goods were exported to Africa and exchanged for slaves who were put to work in the plantations. They were transported to America in such sickening conditions that 1.4 million of the total 11 million slaves died on the voyage.

The more he learnt about it, the more distressed Wilberforce became. He was slow to take up the cause himself, looking for someone more distinguished, but at the prompting of his friend Pitt he became the champion of the anti-slavery movement in 1787. More than two hundred English ships were engaged in the trade, which raided African villages and took men, women and children off in chains. The slaves were packed in layers below decks for the long slow voyage across the Atlantic, where they struggled to endure the stench and filth of the hold before being auctioned to work on the sugar plantations beneath the overseer's whip. But such was the blinding effect of custom that even good men saw no harm in the trade. Whitefield himself had bought slaves for his orphanage in Georgia, to the great disapproval of Wesley. At all events, Wilberforce and some of his friends in the Clapham Sect, to whom we shall turn in a moment, set themselves to get this inhuman trade abolished. Wilberforce met prolonged and fanatical opposition from Parliament, the king, the merchants, the planters and the cities of Bristol and Liverpool, which had grown rich on the trade. But after twenty years he had his reward. In 1807 the slave trade was made illegal in Britain, and in 1833, three days before his death, he had the joy of hearing that all slaves were to be emancipated and slavery banished from the British empire.

He had set out in politics with two aims: to end the slave trade and to improve the morals of the country. He succeeded better in the former than the latter, but his courageous persistence in the face of continuous opposition led to his recognition as one of the greatest Christian humanitarian heroes this country has ever produced.

The Clapham channel

In some parts of the country the evangelical cause was growing. Their churches were full and their mid-week Bible studies and prayer meetings well attended. The time had come when a decisive test was needed. Had the Awakening merely led to personal salvation for countless individuals or was it going to change the face of society? The answer came from Clapham, then a leafy village some three miles from London.

We have already seen how Wilberforce applied his faith in the social and political realm. He was not alone, but just one of a remarkable group of influential laymen who lived in Clapham and were passionate about their Christian faith. There was Henry Thornton MP, the banker, Charles Grant, chairman of the East India Company, James Stephen, a famous lawyer, Zachary Macaulay, who had been Governor of Sierra Leone, Hannah More, the reformer, Lord Teignmouth, who had been Governor-General of India, and others. It was a most distinguished group of Christian leaders and soon earned the nickname of the 'Clapham Sect'. It was easy for scoffers to point to their wealth, their large houses and their influence among the upper classes. But their detractors knew nothing of the extremely disciplined and sacrificial lives they lived. All of them gave to charity far more of their income than they kept for themselves. All of them were scrupulously honest, generous to a fault and determined to show the fruit of their faith in their lives. They were early risers, and most of them spent at least two hours a morning in prayer and Bible study with their Lord. They really loved each other, and there was a fair amount of inter-marriage in this remarkable group, over which the Rector of Clapham, John Venn, exercised a gentle pastoral care.

What they achieved in England was astonishing. They set up lending libraries, established and financed hospitals, sponsored smallpox vaccinations, began schools for the poor, the blind and the deaf, paid for the release of imprisoned debtors, and a great deal more. They set up a Society for the Prevention of Cruelty to Animals, and attempted other moral reforms such as legislation against adultery, Sunday newspapers, lewd-ness, profanity and drunkenness. These had little effect at the time but they did pave the way for further moral advance in the Victorian period.

A significant aspect of their work happened almost by accident. The poet Hannah More was very much a member of the group, although she lived in Somerset. Wilberforce went to visit her. He was staggered by the poverty and depravity of the mining communities in the Mendip hills. The vicar of Cheddar lived in London, his curate in Wells. The thirteen adjoining parishes had no clergy, and the only vicar in the area was celebrated for his drunkenness and fighting. They agreed something had to be done. Wilberforce found money. Hannah and her sisters started a school in a small house in Cheddar. They went to church with the children and held a Bible class for the parents. Despite fierce opposition their admirable initiative spread, not only among the Mendip communities but more widely in the country as a whole. Meanwhile the absentee curate of Cheddar resigned and his successor came to live in the village.

Overseas the achievements of these friends at Clapham were no less significant. They played a major part in the founding of Freetown in Sierra Leone. It was the first British colony in Africa and it was established with three aims: 'the abolition of the slave trade, the civilisation of Africa, and the introduction of the gospel'. They founded the British and Foreign Bible Society, spurred on by a fifteen-year-old Welsh girl, Mary Jones, who was desperate to have a Bible in her own language. After saving up halfpennies for eight years she had walked twenty-five miles barefoot over the mountains to Bala in order to try to buy one. The Clapham Sect also founded the Church Missionary

Society in 1799, of which we shall have more to say in the following pages. In 1809 they set up the London Society for Promoting Christianity among Jews, then what later became known as the Colonial and Continental Church Society to meet the spiritual needs in Newfoundland, and finally the Church Pastoral Aid Society, designed to serve the urban needs thrown up by the Industrial Revolution. The CPAS, comprising both lay and ordained personnel, became particularly effective, and remains so to this day.

This is only a fraction of their achievement. They founded a monthly review called *The Christian Observer*, which was better produced and sold more cheaply than any other journal of the day. They produced attractive tracts at a price no other publishers could match. They wrote books such as Wilberforce's *Real Christianity* and Hannah More's *Thoughts on the Manners of the Great*, both of which had enormous sales. In short, the Clapham Sect changed the face of England: their influence was a mighty healing stream in Britain and beyond.

The Simeon channel

Charles Simeon created a stream of Christian faith which spread across the world, while in England his influence outshone that of any archbishop. Born in Reading in 1759, he was educated at Eton and went up to King's College, Cambridge, as a wild undergraduate, well known for his extravagance in dress and love of horses. The Awakening had passed Cambridge by, and the standards of education, morals and discipline in the university had sunk very low. But three days after his arrival Simeon was informed by the Provost that, in pursuance of some ancient rule, he must receive Holy Communion in chapel three weeks later. He knew enough to realise two things. One, that Communion was a serious matter, and the other that he was utterly unworthy and unprepared. So he acquired a book by Bishop Wilson on the Lord's Supper, which led to the transformation of his life. There he learnt that Jesus had made atonement for his sins, and that he was risen from the grave and alive. He entrusted his whole life to Christ, and immediately the results began to be seen. He took the services in chapel very seriously, though they were often badly rendered. He began to study the Scriptures, to pray and to conform his life to the teaching of Christ. He was entirely alone in all this: there was no Holy Club in Cambridge.

He became a fellow of King's and was ordained in 1782, and the following year was made vicar of Holy Trinity Church in the very heart of the city. The congregation had wanted someone else and made his life a misery. For years the box pews in the nave of the church, paid for by the rich, were locked against him and he had to preach to the side-aisles, which rapidly became very full. For more than ten years most of his congregation had to stand. Rowdy bands of students tried to break up the services, and there were often riots as Simeon emerged from church. But he remained courteous and persistent, and in due course became tolerated and then recognised as the best preacher in Cambridge. He had a profound reverence for Scripture, and in his preaching sought always to proclaim what he believed was in the mind of the Holy Spirit who inspired it. He wrote a commentary on the whole Bible, published invaluable sermon outlines and, although not by nature an early riser, he trained himself to get up at 4.00 a.m. in order to have ample time for his devotions. He held distinguished office in King's, as Dean, Bursar and Vice-Provost, but made time for weekly Friday tea parties in his rooms, to discuss questions of the faith with the large number of undergraduates who turned up. He also ran informal doctrinal evenings from time to time, and especially his famous sermon class in which most of the evangelical preachers of the next generation were trained. This continued for more than fifty years! Simeon moulded the lives of the men from whom the bulk of the English clergy came to be drawn. His influence would be hard to exaggerate.

But Simeon was not content to labour in Cambridge alone, or even England alone. His concern for bringing the gospel to India can be traced back to within four years of taking over Holy Trinity. It continued for the rest of his life. For some years the Eclectic Society, composed of young evangelical clergy whom he gathered together, had been debating how the gospel could be brought to Botany Bay, Africa and the East Indies. But early in 1799, while the French Revolutionary Wars were raging, Simeon posed three crucial questions to his fellow Eclectics which required an answer. They were: 'What can we do? When shall we do it? How shall we do it?' They resolved to found a society immediately, for 'missions to Africa and the East'. The plans were, somewhat surprisingly, approved by church leaders, and in April 1799 the Church Missionary Society was formed by a mere twenty-five people, under Simeon's guidance, with John Venn as chairman and Thornton as treasurer.

In the Church of England there was no precedent for this kind of thing. Inevitably early mistakes were made. But Simeon realised that the best way forward was to get young evangelical clergy appointed as chaplains to the East India Company who would both minister to the whites and begin to reach out to the Indians.

A succession of young men went out, of whom the most famous was Henry Martyn, Senior Wrangler (top mathematics undergraduate at Cambridge University) of his year and fellow of his college. He was preparing for a career at the bar when he chanced to hear a sermon by Charles Simeon about the pioneering work of William Carey in India. This led Martyn to ordination and a chaplaincy in the East India Company. It was a very costly decision because it meant he never married Lydia Grenfell, with whom he was deeply in love. He was a brilliant linguist, rapidly becoming skilled in Sanskrit, Persian and Arabic. He translated the New Testament into Hindustani, Urdu and Persian, and he died of fever in 1812 at the age of thirty-one. His motto was 'Let me burn out for God.' Burn out he did, and his life has been an inspiration ever since, not least to Cambridge undergraduates, whose central meeting place for prayer continues to be the Henry Martyn Hall.

India was not the only overseas concern of Simeon and his friends in the Clapham Sect. Missionaries began to travel to Canada, the Cape, Sierra Leone and New Zealand, and to work among the convicts in Botany Bay in Australia. It is no exaggeration to say that most of the Anglican Communion — the international association of churches around the world that are joined to the Church of England — was brought into being, directly or indirectly, by the Church Missionary Society, and by the man whose three pregnant questions in the Eclectic Society in 1799 led to its inauguration.

There is one other area in Charles Simeon's ministry which has had abiding consequences. It is the Simeon Trust. He had been troubled for many years to see really godly men like Romaine and Newton remaining unbeneficed almost to the end of their lives, while so many of the clergy were ineffective. He determined to do something about it. Some money had been left to him at his brother's death, and he used it to buy up the right to appoint a clergyman as rector of a parish. 'Others purchase income,' he wrote, 'but I purchase spheres of work.' Friends and supporters produced further funding, and the Simeon Trustees now, two hundred years later, look after the appointments to more than a hundred parishes, many of them highly significant. I had the privilege of working as rector of one of them, St Aldate's Church, Oxford. Simeon insisted in his trust deed that those appointed should be truly godly men, of independent mind, and should be dedicated to the welfare of their parishioners. This was a brilliant move, ensuring the continuity of biblical preaching and pastoral care. What a legacy from this man whose ministry contributed so greatly to the healing steams which sprang from the Great Awakening.

The Shaftesbury channel

It is fascinating to trace the way this spiritual renewal in England developed. First there were the fathers under Wesley and Whitefield who pioneered the Awakening. Then the sons, the Clapham Sect. And now the one outstanding Victorian reformer who carried on their work with amazing dedication and effectiveness. Almost all the best of Christian philanthropy during Victoria's reign can be attributed to this remarkable individual who earned the name 'the Poor Man's Earl'. Although he lived rather later than the Clapham friends (1801–85) it is worth glancing at some of his achievements if we are to see where the broadening river of spiritual advance outlined in this chapter led. One of the biggest crowds ever seen in London attended his funeral in Westminster Abbey. His son recalled the scene.

When I saw the crowd which lined the streets, the halt, the blind, the maimed, the poor and the naked standing bare-headed in their rags amidst a pelting rain, to show their love and reverence to their departed friend, I thought it the most heart-stirring sight my eyes had ever looked upon; and I could only feel how happy was the man to whom it had been given to be thus useful in his life and thrice blessed in his death, and to be laid at last to his long sleep amidst the sob of a great nation's heart.

What had this man done to earn his country's gratitude?

He was born Lord Anthony Ashley Cooper, in a loveless aristocratic home where his parents saw little of him. But his early years were enriched by the care of a wonderful maid, Maria Millis. She had clearly been reached by the Awakening and she loved the lad, taught him the stories of the Bible and how to pray, and led his young heart to Christ. While still at Harrow, aged only fifteen, he saw something which fired his faith and ignited his social conscience. Five drunkards were lurching up the street, yelling and carrying a rough coffin of the sort used only for paupers. One of them stumbled. The coffin fell to the ground. They swore. Ashley was horrified. A fellow human being was to be buried, with nobody to mourn him, his remains degraded by drunken men who cared nothing. He resolved to devote his life, as he put it, 'in the cause of the weak, the helpless, both man and beast, and those who had none to help them'. This resolve led him to a life in politics.

His concerns were shared by few if any of his fellow Tories, but he endured their opposition and scorn as he pressed ahead with a stream of reforms in Parliament.

First it was the case of those suffering from mental illnesses. They received no treatment for their illness, but were laid on straw in their asylums and shackled in bed each weekend so that they had to wallow in their own excrement. On Mondays they were washed down in cold water without soap, and one towel sufficed for 160 of them! Ashley succeeded in bringing about reform and proper inspection of asylums.

He then turned his attention to rectifying the worst abuses brought about by the Industrial Revolution. Children as young as five had to work in the factories for fourteen hours a day. Children of six spent all day, and sometimes all night, down the mines. This was intolerable to his Christian conscience and, despite the opprobrium it brought him, he was able to see Acts of Parliament passed which outlawed such practices. But it took all of twenty years!

Throughout his long life we find him standing up for the poor and marginalised. Small boys used to be stripped naked and sent up chimneys to clean them. He got that stopped. He discovered that children were forced to work long hours in the fields for wealthy land-owners, while others were put to work in the brickfields. This too he was able to get rectified. He inaugurated ragged schools — charitable schools offering free education — for the poorest children, staffed by volunteers. Some of his efforts, such as universal education for children, failed because of continued opposition, but it is safe to say no single man has done more for the bettering of the conditions in society than Lord Ashley, or the Earl of Shaftesbury, as he became after 1851 when his father died.

All of this was the outworking of his strong evangelical faith. He proclaimed himself 'an evangelical of the evangelicals'. As such he presided over the Bible Society and brought about legislation which allowed mission services to be held in unconsecrated buildings: the crowds which flocked to the Exeter Hall, and later to rallies in theatres, showed what a successful attempt this was to reach the non-churchgoer. It was Shaftesbury who backed the Missions to Seamen, the London City Mission, the Church's ministry among the Jews, the Open Air Mission and the YMCA and YWCA. Through his friendship with Palmerston, the prime minister, he was able to end the scandalous practice of choosing bishops on political and social grounds, and ensure the appointment of men of real faith and godliness to positions of leadership.

Shaftesbury's astonishing life's work was a major tributary of that river of spiritual life, originating in the

Great Awakening a hundred years earlier, which now began to fertilise the whole country.

What are we to learn of the hand of God in this developing stream of healthy Christianity? There are many lessons for us, just as there were many men and women involved. It all begins with a personal surrender to Jesus Christ and the welcome of his Spirit into the heart. It is nourished by a strong devotional life. It affects relationships. It evokes compassion for those less fortunate. It drives men and women out in sacrificial service to others. It seeks to 'build Jerusalem among those dark Satanic mills'. It reminds us that a Christianity which does not begin with the individual does not begin, but a Christianity which ends with the individual ends.

6

Floods in the valleys
The Welsh revival

As the nineteenth century drew towards its close, the familiar tendency to spiritual decline after great spiritual advance once again appeared.

Politically, Britain was the foremost power in the world, but with power came corruption. Corruption in the way she handled some − not all − of the subject peoples in her empire. Corruption in morals, so prim and proper on the outside but frequently so immoral on the inside. The very phrase 'Victorian religion and morality' has an unpleasant taste because it is so closely associated with hypocrisy. Despite all the reforms Lord Shaftesbury had brought in, the lot of the poor was terrible. Their labour was shamefully exploited in the factories. The peasants in the countryside eked out a miserable living. And nowhere was the situation more dire than in the little principality of Wales. And yet, in 1904, there was for a few months an amazing explosion of God's transforming power. To pursue the analogy of springs in the desert, it was like a fresh geyser bursting up in Yellowstone Park in the United States. But it was not without antecedents.

Antecedents to the revival

Wales is a land of passion, be it in singing, religious revivals or rugby football. And in 1858 remarkable news began to percolate through from America. A businessman in New York, Jeremiah Lanphier, sensing the prevailing economic depression of the day, gave out several thousand fliers inviting people to a midday hour of prayer on a Wednesday. On the first occasion he was the only one praying in the little room on the third floor of the church in Fulton Street for much of the hour, but finally he was joined by five other businessmen. The next week there were twenty, and the following week forty. So they determined to meet not just weekly but daily, and soon prayer meetings were springing up all over the city. Before long some fifty thousand people seem to have been involved. Prayer led to blessing, and in 1859 enormous numbers of people came to explicit Christian faith throughout America and Canada, the number estimated at about a million. News of all this reached Wales, and Dafydd Morgan, a Calvinistic Methodist preacher, was profoundly intrigued and longed for a similar outpouring of God's Spirit in Wales. One night in October 1858 he says that he went to bed 'a lamb' and woke up the next morning 'a lion' for the Lord. This led to his engaging in a powerful preaching ministry up and down Wales. A parallel movement of God's Spirit took place not only in England but in many other countries at this time. It was virtually worldwide in this single year, 1859.

Wales was not unused to such eruptions of spiritual vitality. They came and then quite soon they died down. It was as though God picked up one or more people as instruments of his love and life, and then laid them aside again once the demonstration of his power could not be gainsaid. At any rate Dafydd Morgan later returned to being 'a lamb' again, and carried on a faithful but uneventful ministry until his death in 1883.

There were various other tides of spiritual revival in Wales at the end of the nineteenth century, notably in the north led by Richard Owen in the early 1880s, but nothing matched what happened in 1904. It attracted enormous attention not only in the press but abroad, and people came from the continent and as far away as Australia to see what was happening. This is all the more remarkable since it was mainly confined to two denominations, the Calvinistic Methodists and the Congregationalists, and took place largely in the mining valleys of South Wales. Moreover, the language of this revival was Welsh. It had little effect among English-speaking people or within most of the (Anglican) Church in Wales. And yet it made such an impact that still in Wales today, a century and more later, they look back wistfully to 'the Revival'.

An unpromising situation

It seems that these 'springs in the desert' tend to take place at a time when spiritual life is low and either scepticism or opposition is rife. At the beginning of the 1900s Wales was spiritually bankrupt. Several factors combined to bring about low church attendance, low morals and low expectations, but possibly the most significant was the rise of liberal theology.

This was highlighted by the publication in 1860 of *Essays and Reviews*, which caused a big stir. It argued the need for unfettered enquiry in religion. Gradually the implications of Charles Darwin's *Origin of Species* impacted the theological schools of the day. The concept of God's revelation in Scripture began to give way to the evolution of religious ideas. Emphasis was laid on the humanity rather than the deity of Christ, and the moral influence of the cross was stressed rather than its vicarious power. Closely associated with this change in the theological climate was the German Higher Criticism of the Bible, so that it was no longer seen as God's word to humanity but rather as humanity's words about God. This was also the period when psychology was taking root and attracting a large following. One of the leading exponents was William James. He did not give much credence to the seriousness of human sin or the objective nature of the atonement. Instead, as his celebrated book *The Varieties of Religious Experience* argued, conversion was best seen as a normal and temporary adolescent phenomenon, springing from subconscious emotional excitement. There is plenty of evidence in the church papers and theological essays of the time to show that these views had penetrated deeply into the training of Welsh pastors and even into the teaching of the Sunday schools. The religious climate was cold, and few could have expected the revival which soon swept the country.

Underground streams

However, in every period of spiritual decline there are faithful people ardent in prayer to God for a change. It was so in Elijah's day, when he thought that he was the last prophet of a doomed religion but learnt to his amazement that there were seven thousand in Israel who had not bowed the knee to Baal. In Wales, too, a prophetic figure emerged: David Howell, an Anglican clergyman who was Dean of St David's Cathedral. He was a man of great warmth and broad sympathies, who was deeply committed to the truths of the New Testament and much respected and loved throughout the land. In December 1902 he had written an important article in a Welsh journal describing the spiritual situation as he saw it. The preaching was competent but lacked passion and divine anointing – there was 'no smiting of the conscience, no laying bare the condition of the soul as in times past'. The authority of the

Bible and the fundamental truths of Christianity were 'weighed in the balance of reason and criticism as though they were nothing more than human opinions'. He believed that 'a Holy Spirit religion is the only cure for the moral and spiritual disease of Wales at this time'. He appealed to all to 'create a circle of implorers' who would make 'a revival of religion the chief end of their desire'. He concluded with a passage which touched hearts throughout the country.

Take note. If it were known that this was my last message to my fellow countrymen, throughout the length and breadth of Wales, before being summoned to the judgment, the light of eternity already breaking over me, it would be that the principal need of my country and dear nation at present is still spiritual revival through a special outpouring of the Holy Spirit.

Within a month he had died.

But just as there are always underground rumblings before a volcano erupts, so there were other indications that something powerful was about to happen. A series of five articles in a Congregational weekly during 1904, based on widespread consultation among ministers, pointed out that prayer always has a prominent part in every awakening, that these awakenings may differ in character, that local efforts are usually crucial, and that there are dangers as well as advantages in such awakenings. The topic of revival was now on the agenda of most denominational gatherings, and spontaneous prayer meetings had been springing up around the country. For example, four young eighteen-year-olds were found on a mountainside in Glamorganshire pleading with God for revival in their church — and it transpired that these young men had been holding their prayer meeting every night on the mountain for a month past. When this prayer circle became known, others joined it, including some who never went to church. Before long there were scores, then hundreds — largely consisting of young people. There is evidence of an extensive prayer movement in many parts of Wales, including the mining communities of the Rhondda Valley where the 1904 revival would soon break out in power. This prayer was not centrally organised in any way: it was a spontaneous and widespread longing for God to reverse the spiritual decline in the land.

The floodwaters of revival

That same spontaneity was a significant mark of the revival itself. It is hard to say just when it began. It did not depend on the ministry of particular individuals, though several were prominent. The power of the Holy Spirit broke out without any human agency in place after place. But perhaps February 1904 is the date, and the little coastal village of New Quay the place to begin. Joseph Jenkins was minister of the Calvinistic Methodist Church in New Quay. He worked closely with his nephew John Thickens, the minister in nearby Aberaeron. The two men could hardly have been more different. Thickens was balanced and studious, Jenkins erratic and at times very strict. But they both had the same hunger to see more of God's blessing in the Church, and both were very disturbed by the current loss of fervour in the chapels and growth of secular organisations and preoccupations among the people. They also recognised that they themselves needed a fresh touch of God on their lives.

Crucial conventions

When on holiday in Llandrindod Wells the previous year, they had stumbled upon a convention on biblical holiness which helped them a great deal. It was the Welsh offshoot of the Keswick Convention, a large annual gathering in the Lake District to promote holiness. Soon the effect was seen in their ministries, especially among the young people in their churches. One young woman in New Quay, Florrie Evans, was unsure of her salvation, and went for counsel to her pastor, Joseph Jenkins. Shortly afterwards he added a new feature to his large youth meeting: there was to be opportunity for individuals to give public testimony to God's work in their lives. The first time he launched this, on 14 February 1904, there was a long silence and then Florrie Evans broke out, 'I love the Lord Jesus with all my heart.' This was the catalyst for an amazing time of blessing among the young people of New Quay, in which two other young women, Maud Davies and May Phillips, were set ablaze spiritually. Person after person then rose to profess wholehearted surrender to Christ. One eyewitness in that youth meeting wrote, 'It was the beginning of the visible manifestation of the Spirit breaking out in life-streams which afterwards would touch thousands.' News of this remarkable youth meeting spread widely in the vicinity and led to young people testifying in other churches. The original trio of Florrie Evans, Maud Davies and May Phillips were all influential later in the revival.

In September 1904 the Revd Seth Joshua, a dynamic preacher who had been set aside as evangelist for the Presbyterian Church, arrived at New Quay for a mission. He too had been moved and his spirituality deepened by the 'Keswick Convention' meetings in Llandrindod. But he was not uncritical of the convention's teaching. He felt that Keswick was too rigid in the steps it laid down for achieving God's blessing, and that it concentrated too much on holiness in believers to the detriment of reaching out with the gospel to unbelievers. When he came to New Quay he could see that God was already very much at work. This gave him a platform for a very successful mission. The presence of the Holy Spirit in the meetings was palpable. The singing, prayers, testimonies and exhortations were electric. The meetings were closed two or three times, but others would cry out for mercy or break out in joyful thanksgiving. Seth

Joshua sensed that revival was on the way. He then moved on to Newcastle Emlyn, accompanied by fifteen of the enthusiastic youth from New Quay. Seth Joshua preached powerfully but felt the spiritual ground was hard. The response was limited, but it was here that Evan Roberts, a young man of twenty-six who was to become extremely influential in the revival, first heard Joshua and was deeply impressed.

Evan Roberts

Newcastle Emlyn was where the Calvinistic Methodists did the initial training of their ministers. Among them was Evan Roberts. He had long been a serious lad and a devout Christian, spending several hours a day in Bible study. He lived in the village of Loughor and had joined his father working down the mine at the age of eleven until he was twenty-three, and then in 1902 he became apprenticed to a blacksmith before giving in to the urge to be ordained. He joined the training college in 1904. Joshua had long been unhappy at the heavy emphasis on academic study in the theological colleges, and had been praying that God would raise up a miner to be an evangelist. It soon became evident that Evan Roberts was that man.

Joshua, Jenkins and others, including Roberts, went from Newcastle Emlyn to Blaenannerch, a small village near Cardigan, where a further conference had been planned. During one of the prayer meetings, Roberts burst out with a heartfelt prayer as he reflected on God's great love. He was in agony of soul. His face was bathed in sweat and he cried out, 'Bend me, bend us. Bend us!'

This outburst caused a great stir, but it became almost a motto of the revival — 'Bend the Church and save the world.' At all events Roberts was filled with peace after this experience, but also with an all-consuming sense of responsibility to preach the love of God throughout Wales. He surrendered himself fully to the Holy Spirit, and was given a profound conviction that no fewer than a hundred thousand people would be won for Christ.

Roberts soon became the key person in the revival, though, as we saw earlier, no individuals could claim leadership of the movement. It broke out apparently at random in late 1904 and early 1905 wherever people were praying and longing for a fresh touch of God's power. But Roberts was an important part of it. This is all the more remarkable because he had received little education, had worked down the mines for eleven years, and had only just started at the theological school at Newcastle Emlyn. He decided that he could not remain in training: he must get on with the ministry which he felt God had laid upon him. So he left the college and returned to his home village of Loughor.

This seemed very strange to his family, who naturally regarded his highly emotional religious state with suspicion. But Evan was no ordinary minister in training. He was something of a mystic and often had overwhelming visions which directed the course of his ministry. He saw them as a fulfilment of Joel 2:28, 'Your young men will see visions.' If we are to understand the intensity of the revival it will help to glance at one or two of these visions, especially as he frequently referred to them. In one of them he saw multitudes going down an incline towards the bottomless pit of hell. In anguish he cried to God to close hell's door for one year so that they might have opportunity to respond. On another occasion he saw a hand, which he took to be God's, holding a piece of paper with the number 100,000 on it. On another, when depressed, he had a picture of Satan laughing with contempt, only to be met by a glorious figure clothed in white and bearing a flaming sword which banished the devil. His return to Loughor was also prompted by a vision of his old companions in the village sitting before him, and a voice saying to him, 'Go and speak to these people.' Despite the misunderstanding his return would involve, he obeyed.

After a difficult start, Roberts began to see the fruit for which he longed. His brother and three sisters came to a lively faith and started family prayers. The youth meetings in Loughor and nearby Gorseinon grew in numbers and impact and rapidly drew public attention. Before long he was preaching to hundreds.

As a result the *Western Mail* sent a journalist to report on one of the meetings. He was much impressed. Here is part of his report.

The preacher did not remain in his seat. For the most part he walked up and down the aisles, open Bible in hand, exhorting one, encouraging another, and kneeling with a third to implore a blessing from the Throne of Grace. A young woman rose to give out a hymn, which was sung with deep earnestness. While it was being sung several people dropped down in their seats as if they had been struck, and commenced crying for pardon. Then from another part of the chapel could be heard the voice of a young man reading a portion of scripture. Finally Mr Roberts announced the holding of future meetings, and at 4.25 (a.m.!) the gathering dispersed.

Although the nightly meetings often stretched into the small hours, the *Western Mail* was covering every one. This publicity by a major Welsh daily undoubtedly contributed to the celebrity and impact of the revival, and the crowds of visitors who came to experience it.

When Roberts preached, it was in a quiet, intense voice, very different from the fire-and-brimstone style of many revivalists. But on the whole Evan Roberts did little preaching. He left the meeting entirely in the hands of the Spirit, and song, testimonies, shouting, visions and verses of Scripture followed one another with no discernible plan. Often the meeting was begun by some of the young women who had accompanied him from New Quay. They launched into personal confession and passionate prayer, while Roberts was on his knees in the aisle urging people to repent and surrender to Christ. I once had the chance to talk to a very old man who had, as a small boy, crept into one of these meetings to see what was going on. His verdict? 'Mad, quite mad.' So it must have seemed as men and women were convulsed with tears of repentance, writhed on the floor or shouted with joy once they were assured of God's forgiveness.

There was now no question of returning to the ministry training college in Newcastle Emlyn. Roberts was on the road wherever he sensed the Spirit calling him, but refused to go anywhere unless he had that inner conviction. Other people naturally thought this subjective understanding of guidance was strange and rude. But Evan insisted that all his moves were the direct result of the Holy Spirit's guidance. Thus in the winter of 1904 he traversed much of Welsh-speaking South Wales, particularly the valleys of the Rhondda, where, in addition to constant meetings in church, he would stand at the mine head at 5.00 a.m. inviting the night shift to come to the evening meetings. Often he would go down the mine itself and pray with the miners, with amazing results.

One interesting aspect of this great awakening was that it did not depend on Roberts or the presence of any of the leading figures in the revival. This seemed to be the sovereign work of God in the principality. It grew spontaneously. As the news spread, churches took their faith more seriously, ministers were revitalised, their preaching became more challenging, and the work went on without human planning, spreading to North Wales early in 1905.

Four steps to blessing

Evan Roberts would constantly teach that there were four definite steps needed for the 'baptism of the Holy Spirit'. He saw this as a second critical stage in the Christian life, an instantaneous experience subsequent to conversion. This view influenced the emerging Pentecostals both in Britain and America, although there were no 'tongues' associated with the experience in Wales. The four steps were as follows. First, the past must be cleaned up by confession to God and putting right any wrong done to others. Second, every doubtful thing in life must be put away. Third, there must be prompt and wholehearted obedience to the Holy Spirit. And fourth, there must be fearless public confession of Christ. These points were emphasised by others leading the movement. They saw it as a return to the first Pentecost when Peter urged his hearers to repent, which involved a changed attitude to God and restitution for wrongs done to others. The promise was then full remission of sins and the gift of the Holy Spirit to come and possess the disciples and give them the courage to become public and fearless witnesses to Jesus.

Although he was not much of a preacher, Roberts did emphasise biblical authority, and was willing to test his visions by their conformity to Scripture. He set out to get his Christian hearers, often backslidden, right with God first, and then to see them 'baptised with the Holy Spirit', the critical experience that would issue in what was called 'the overcoming life', that is to say a life of habitual victory over habitual moral failures. All of this regularly took place during extended meetings in the context of passionate prayer and ecstatic praise. This was a 'singing revival', and its impact was for a while irresistible. Statistics show that the 100,000 figure was indeed reached within the year, some 24,000 new members being added to the Calvinistic Methodist Church, 26,500 to the Presbyterians, 4,000 to the Wesleyans and the rest distributed between the Baptists and the Church in Wales. It was an astonishing outpouring of God's Holy Spirit, directed not by people but by that same divine Spirit.

Collapse

Opposition

Needless to say, a phenomenon of this magnitude attracted opposition.

The Revd Peter Price, a Congregationalist minister, launched an unbridled attack in the columns of the *Western Mail* in January 1905, and a heated and prolonged public debate ensued. Price maintained there were two revivals, one — such as he had witnessed in his own church over the past two years — 'gloriously real'. The other, in which Evan Roberts was involved, he denounced as sham and a blasphemous travesty of the real thing. Price, who was a Cambridge-educated pastor, had two main objections. One was to Evan Roberts' claim to be under the direct and sustained control of the Holy Spirit. The other was his complete rejection of the emotionalism and the physical manifestations which accompanied the meetings of the revival.

The revivalists, he thought, were tarred with the Montanist brush, a somewhat heretical charismatic movement in the second century AD which majored on prophetic utterances and visions, much as Roberts did, and, like him, gathered an enormous following. This charge hurt Roberts deeply, although he declined to reply to it. Indeed, it marked a turning-point in his ministry, because it led him to make even more passionate claims to direct inspiration by the Spirit. This was a serious problem: in one meeting he cried out in agony that a damned soul was present. It was no good to pray for him, Roberts asserted, for he was finally damned. This incident made it clear to many that Roberts was becoming deranged.

Withdrawal

Evan Roberts became a nervous wreck as early as February 1905, and never again engaged in solo public ministry. Instead, he became something of a recluse, and gave himself to prayer for worldwide revival until his death in 1951. He never married and was never ordained. He remains an outstanding example of a most unlikely man raised up to usher in a mighty movement of the Spirit of God, and then being laid aside after it was over.

The weaknesses of the revival

The revival had enormous strengths. Thousands of homes were transformed by the conversion of whole families. The churches were renewed, and they impacted society as never before. The gospel became the main topic of conversation throughout the nation for several months, and people came from all over the world to see what was happening. Unfortunately, however, the weaknesses of the movement were as evident as its strengths. We must glance at three of them.

Roberts' breakdown and obsession with demons

The main thrust of the movement collapsed when Evan Roberts broke down in 1905 and never fully recovered. Was he neurotic? Had his nerves given out because he had lived on them for a year with insufficient rest and sleep? Was his claim to live in constant contact with and obedience to the Holy Spirit credible in the light of his increasingly erratic behaviour?

Or was there something worse? Was the devil at work in the revival, and should many of its manifestations, in Roberts as in others, be assigned to demonic activity? This last was much discussed, especially as Jessie Penn-Lewis, an untrained and unbalanced leader in the revival, took him under her roof for a couple of years to convalesce. In all he stayed there eight years and together they wrote a book, *War on the Saints*, which asserted that unprecedented Satanic activity had been aroused by the revival, that the tribulations of the book of Revelation were upon them, and that the world would end in 1913. In this book Roberts admitted demonic activity in his meetings – an admission he later retracted. At all events, his obsession with demons was disastrous, and the revival seems to have come to a screeching halt with his emotional and physical break-down. It had exercised an unparalleled impact on the country, but had lasted less than a year.

Emotionalism

True religion often touches the emotions. But playing on the emotions is a recipe for disaster. Unfortunately there was plenty of this in the revival. The charge of emotionalism was just. This was where the revival differed so sharply from that of 1859, where strong teaching had been the major instrument in renewal. In 1904 there was no clearly defined biblical teaching. Preaching did not play a great part in the meetings. Converts were not properly followed up and consequently many of them lapsed. Welsh chapelgoers became accustomed to looking for occasional and emotional showers of blessing from God rather than steady growth through Bible reading, prayer, church attendance, the sacraments and abiding in Christ.

Doctrinal aberrations

There were serious doctrinal weaknesses in the movement. Roberts taught that it was essential, if you wanted a victorious Christian life, to have a second experience of the Holy Spirit after conversion. This followed full repentance and the bending of the human will to total obedience, and it was ushered in by hours of crying to the Holy Spirit to 'come, come now, come with increasing power'. This inevitably led to abuse, and people were given to understand that a whole new dimension of life, 'entire sanctification' or 'the higher life', would be theirs after this power-encounter with the Spirit, rather like stepping into a lift and being transported to the top floor of the building, whereas the ordinary Christian had to climb doggedly up the stairs! However, the main teaching of the New Testament speaks of the daily dying to sin and claiming Christ's resurrection power, and of the struggle to apprehend the goals for which we have been apprehended by Christ. So a good deal of the teaching about the Holy Spirit in the revival has to be suspect.

Roberts operated entirely by what he believed the Holy Spirit was telling him to do. He would not be swayed by human advice offered even by his most spiritual friends. But there is great danger in this virtual claim to unfailing divine inspiration and guidance, not least because it can lead to stubborn independence of other people, to wild decisions and to confusing the Spirit's promptings with one's own ideas or with demonic interference. This was certainly the case with Roberts, as his later tragic career showed. Moreover, the constant plea in revival meetings for a fresh 'baptism in the Spirit', a second crisis for believers, is never used in that way in the New Testament, where the seven times the phrase occurs all refer to the initial reception of the Spirit when a person becomes a Christian, not to a new level of Christian experience for believers.

However, it would be churlish to concentrate only on the weaknesses of this remarkable movement of God's Spirit. Let us turn to its strengths.

The strengths of the revival

Worldwide impact

This was the greatest spiritual awakening ever recorded in Wales. Not only did it reach throughout the principality, but it created ripples much further afield. There are accounts of other contemporary revivals in many parts of the world which were triggered by the events in Wales. The Welsh exiles in Patagonia had much the same experience, and when Seth Joshua visited America in 1906 similar outbursts of spiritual refreshment broke out and launched the Pentecostal movement

The British prime minister, David Lloyd George, spoke with great enthusiasm of the revival and mentioned its spread to places as far afield as Paris and Naples. Norway and Sweden caught the flame, and so did many parts of Africa and even Australia and New Zealand. The Welsh missionaries in northeast India witnessed a remarkable revival in 1905, and Amy Carmichael, the well-known missionary at Dohnavur in southwest India, writes of a similar visitation among the unemotional Tamils. There the intensity of prayer, the melting of hard hearts, the desire to follow the lead of the Spirit wholeheartedly, the tears, and the joy of Christian assurance, were unprecedented. It would not be too much to say that the Welsh revival of 1904 contributed significantly to the growth of the Church worldwide during the following decade, and that while missionaries were involved, most of the blessing fell among the indigenous people themselves. They experienced a new unity, a greater desire to spread the gospel, and fresh joy and assurance. Undeniably, countless lives were transformed.

Personal and social transformation

But of course the impact was not merely numerical, and cannot be evaluated by what took place in various parts of the world in the wake of the 1904 revival. If it did not make significant difference to the lifestyle of the Welsh people, we would have every reason to discount it as mere emotionalism. But enormous numbers of radically changed lives emerged. Down the mines the pit ponies could no longer understand their masters because of the absence of oaths and curses! The sales of beer plummeted, and pubs went out of business as thousands of men became teetotal. Convictions for drunkenness were halved. Crime diminished. Well-known drunkards and prize fighters were to be found praying and giving their testimony at the nightly meetings which continued to be held in the chapels. Employers were impressed by the increased effort men put into their work. Debts were paid, feuds healed, families bonded together. The social impact of the revival was enormous for a while, though by the end of the Great War it had largely melted away, and today, sadly, there is no sign of it.

Lay leadership

There were other results which gradually affected society at large. One was the liberation of women, since Florrie Evans, Jessie Penn-Lewis and others played a prominent part in the public meetings and in ministry to individuals. They often led meetings, even when ministers were present. The laymen of the churches, too, came into their own. No longer did they merely attend on a Sunday, but the faith was glowing in their hearts, so they prayed together in the mines and on the trains. They formed a close fellowship with one another, and this was one of the major tributaries leading into the socialism which was emerging in Wales and has characterised the country ever since. This was a revival which particularly reached young people. Prayer meetings led by youths sprang up all over the country. At almost every prayer meeting people committed their lives to Christ. The preaching of many clergy, too, was changed. No longer merely correct and formal, it was increasingly directed at the heart and the lifestyle of the hearers.

Prayer, unity and experience

Looking back, other strengths stand out in clear relief. One is that if Christian people are brought into a lively, obedient and prayerful attitude before God, this will prove to be magnetic and the gospel will spread readily among those who are not yet Christians. Another is that prayer is the indispensable prelude to blessing, and that this blessing becomes personal when men and women see the cross of Christ raised high, and are broken down when they realise how much it cost him to win them. Christian unity was a further interesting outcome. Wherever the floodtides of the revival flowed, denominational differences, an ingrained feature in Welsh Christianity, were melted into a new fellowship in Christ. The importance of personal experience in religion is another aspect of the revival, in contrast to the cold churchgoing which so often passes for Christian observance. And it is salutary to reflect that the primary result of the revival was not individual blessings, great as they were, but a changed atmosphere, in which the Holy Spirit was free to work without hindrance. That changed atmosphere included a new awe before God, a new seriousness in religion, a massive improvement in morality, and a much warmer and cohesive family life.

Perhaps the greatest benefit of the revival was the new spiritual dynamism, the new assurance of salvation, the new courage to confess Christ, the new determination to surrender everything to the Lord, which began to characterise many thousands, for the first time in their lives.

The hymn of the revival

You might call the hymn below the signature tune of the revival. It resounded through the valleys. At its core lies profound gratitude for what Jesus achieved at Calvary, the divine grace that will never be forgotten, and that leads to transformed lives, exuberant in praise.

> Here is Love, vast as the ocean,
> Lovingkindness as the flood,
> Where the Prince of Life, our ransom
> Shed for us his precious blood.

Who his love will not remember?
Who can cease to sing his praise?
He can never be forgotten
Throughout heaven's eternal days.

On the mount of crucifixion
Fountains opened deep and wide;
Through the floodgates of God's mercy
Flowed a vast and gracious tide.
Grace and love, like mighty rivers,
Poured incessant from above,
And heaven's peace and perfect justice
Kissed a guilty world in love.

7

Overflowing the banks
The charismatic movement

The impact of the Welsh revival was felt as far away as America, and Joseph Smales, pastor of First Baptist in Los Angeles, had himself travelled to Wales to witness the phenomenon. His efforts to reproduce something of the sort were fruitless, but hunger for revival was in the air, and the year 1905 saw widespread prayer throughout California for a fresh breath of God's Spirit.

Five years earlier, a woman called Agnes Ozman, student in a tiny Bible school founded by Charles Parham in Kansas, found herself 'praying in tongues' as the clock struck midnight in a Watchnight Service (a late-night service to see in the New Year) on 31 December 1900. Within a few days half the thirty-four students in the school, including Parham himself, were praying in tongues. One of the students was William J. Seymour, a one-eyed African-American son of former slaves. Seymour arrived in Los Angeles in February 1906, and with a small group of followers began to hold meetings in a private home, 214 Bonnie Brae

Street. More of the group found themselves praying in tongues, the worship was ecstatic, and for several days around Easter it was carried on round the clock. The road outside the house was blocked with curious onlookers, and Seymour and his friends realised they needed larger premises. What they found was not much larger! They decamped to 312 Azusa Street, a tumbledown shack of only 60 feet by 40 which had been used for lumber and had then become a stable for horses. Inside, the place was a wreck. It was here in April 1906 that the Pentecostal Church was born. There was a massive eruption of tongues and uninhibited evangelism, which continued for some ten years. Though the core community rarely exceeded fifty, already by May that year fifteen hundred people, old and young, black, white and Hispanic, were struggling to crowd into the building. Needless to say, this attracted nationwide notoriety.

The Pentecostals

And so began the Pentecostal denomination, the fastest growing Christian organisation in the world today. Some of their roots lay in Wesleyan Methodism, where believers were seeking that complete sanctification of which Wesley had written and also a return to the spirituality of the first century when tongues, prophecy, healing and exorcism accompanied the preaching of the gospel. These emerging Pentecostals claimed that speaking in tongues was the initial and decisive mark of the 'the baptism in the Holy Spirit', a view which was firmly rejected by other denominations, including the Wesleyan Methodists. So the Pentecostals started a new denomination of their own. It had many strengths. It was emphatically interracial, and that is remarkable in the year 1906 when racial segregation was at its height. They also encouraged women in leadership, and that was fourteen years before women in America gained the vote. Their meetings were entirely unprogrammed. No musical instruments were used. Indeed, such was the excitement and shouting that none were needed. Their meetings were not advertised, and there was no organisation to back them. Yet they grew prodigiously.

The great weakness of the movement was its sad fragmentation into a whole variety of Pentecostal sub-groups, all of them, however, believing that the gifts of the Holy Spirit as evidenced in the New Testament, particularly tongues, healing, exorcism and prophecy, had not died out but were available today to empower God's people to spread the gospel and live at a new spiritual level. They faced a lot of scorn and opposition, from sceptics and from other Christians alike. Their style of worship appealed particularly, though not exclusively, to the poor, the illiterate, the spiritually unsatisfied, and people looking for an intense spiritual experience and a warm Christian community. However, despite their splits, the

Pentecostals were at one in their assurance that they alone possessed this precious gift, the baptism in the Holy Spirit.

The charismatic movement

But God proved to be less stingy! On 3 April 1960 the Revd Dennis Bennett, the High Church rector of St Mark's Episcopal Church, Van Nuys, California, announced from the pulpit that he had been baptised with the Holy Spirit. This caused enormous media frenzy so, rather than embarrass his church, he resigned and went to St Luke's Episcopal Church, Seattle, where he stayed for twenty years. During this time he not only founded the Episcopal Renewal Ministries with its celebrated journal *Acts 29*, but travelled widely throughout the world speaking about this 'baptism with the Holy Spirit'. I heard him that year, at the English theological college where I was a junior member of staff, and I found it all very disturbing and unbiblical. Years later, however, I visited St Luke's, Seattle, and expected to see fireworks. Not at all. It was a rather dreary Evensong, but with this simple invitation at the end: 'You are welcome to join the prayer meeting afterwards, downstairs in the basement.' I went, and was amazed at the vitality of an extraordinary, packed, multicultural meeting, full of praise, some prophetic utterances and a passion to spread the gospel and minister to the hungry in the streets of Seattle. Perhaps it was not so crazy after all. But I did not realise that when I first heard Bennett in 1960.

The start of the charismatic movement in 1960s Britain

The charismatic movement began in England in the early 1960s, though it soon overflowed all banks and spread across the world and throughout all denominations. It turned out to be yet another gracious and powerful invasion by God into the increasing secularism and hedonism of the mid-twentieth century, a generation that was tired of dogma, suspicious of the words of politicians and preachers, and yet hungry for experience. It was, in some respects, the counterpart of the great cultural change taking place at that time in the secular realm which we call postmodernism.

It is not easy to give a definition of postmodernism, a disparate reaction against the pervading 'modernism' or rationalism that had dominated European thought for the previous two hundred years. It is hard to improve on John Stott's explanation.

In general, modernism proclaims the autonomy of human reason, especially in the cold objectivity of science, whereas postmodernism prefers the warmth of subjective experience. Modernism is committed to the quest for truth, believing that certainty is attainable; postmodernism is committed to pluralism, affirming the validity of all ideologies, and tolerance as the *supreme virtue. Modernism declares the inevitability of social progress; postmodernism pricks the bubble of utopian dreams. Modernism exalts self-centred individualism; but postmodernism seeks the togetherness of community. Modernism is supremely self-confident; whereas postmodernism is humble enough to question everything, for it lacks confidence in anything.*

It is not hard to see that the charismatic movement has significant parallels with postmodernism and speaks powerfully to the postmodern scene. It too was a revolt — against the dryness of evangelical and Anglo-Catholic Christianity. Like postmodernism, it placed a high value on community, and had a disdain for hierarchy and tradition. And like postmodernism it valued experience more than intellectual achievement. Supremely, the charismatic movement was a spiritual revival among the churches, awakening people to the possibility of experiencing the Holy Spirit for themselves, empowering laypeople for service, and bringing joy, love and confidence to a church which in the sixties had its back to the wall as it struggled against scientism, atheism and a new explosive hedonism. This movement provided exactly the right emphasis, in the providence of God, for the times in which it was born. We do not have space to follow its worldwide influence in places like East Africa, Argentina or Korea, but it made an enormous impact in England.

Spontaneous combustion

There was a touch of spontaneous combustion about its spread. The fire of the Holy Spirit's love and power broke out without authorisation by church authorities, without any notable spiritual leader or prophetic figure, and without any respect for denominations. You might have expected the liturgical denominations to be the most resistant. But such was not the case. The charismatic movement profoundly affected the Orthodox, the Anglicans and the Roman Catholics. Pope Leo XIII, standing at the door of the twentieth century, had predicted that it would be a century for the fresh honouring of the Holy Spirit. But even he could hardly have imagined that in 1975 ten thousand fervent charismatic Roman Catholics would be singing in tongues in St Peter's in the presence of his successor, Pope Paul VI. The Pope appointed Cardinal Suenens, himself a charismatic, to foster the movement in the Catholic Church. There were some delightful touches. I know of one celebrated monk who had a serious impediment in his speech. He received the gift of tongues and thereafter became a fluent linguist! Another was when Cardinal Suenens had been leading a university mission in Oxford. I was at that time rector of an Oxford church, and remember him coming to a prayer meeting held in our home on the night the mission finished. He was exhausted, knelt down in the midst of fifty or more of us, mainly undergraduates, and asked us (Protestants) to lay hands upon his head and pray for a new infilling of the Holy Spirit.

The Anglicans had already been impacted by this fresh movement of the Holy Spirit. Michael Harper was filled with the Spirit while a curate at All Souls, Langham Place, and founded the Fountain Trust, which was very influential in the spread of the movement. Congregations led by clergy like John Perry in Chorleywood, John Collins in Gillingham and David Watson in York were rejoicing in newfound joy, love, freedom and experimentation despite inevitably making some early mistakes, such as exaggerated claims for healing or moral perfection. Prebendary John Collins tells me of the special significance the charismatic movement had for working men. 'Some of the meetings in Southampton Town Hall were packed with working-class men just like a football match! They did not merely go to meetings, but were empowered for outreach.' Collins adds, 'The men in the congregation in Gillingham were very helpful to me if I wanted a carpet laid, but I never succeeded in mobilising them in mission until they had had an experience of the Holy Spirit.' It was an exciting time to be a Christian.

I was personally drawn into the movement (of which I had previously been very critical) when ministering in Singapore Cathedral at the invitation of Bishop Chiu Ban It. More of that in a later chapter. Suffice to say that I received the gift of prayer in tongues without asking for it! In apparently unplanned and disorderly ways like this, the good news of the reality of God's love, and the outpouring of his Spirit upon God's sons and daughters, has been spread by clergy and laypeople during the last fifty years. It spread by word of mouth. It spread by people in Bible studies and prayer groups telling of the new joy and power that they had received. It spread as people asked to be prayed for in church after services. It spread in universities and national and international conferences, such as the Fountain Trust and the 1988 Lambeth Conference, as men and women, young and old, tried to keep up with what God was doing. Indeed, at that conference Anglican bishops were to be seen dancing with joy around the high altar at Westminster Abbey!

The charismatic movement in the local church

The biggest impact of the charismatic movement was in local churches which rediscovered the joy and enthusiasm of early Christianity. The most obvious indications to the casual observer would have been new songs, usually led by 'worship groups' rather than the regular choir, and accompanied by guitars and other instruments rather than the organ. This was to emphasise the 'every member ministry' which the charismatics were so keen to stress. The words were often overly subjective and the music undistinguished, but these songs reflected the way charismatics felt impelled to express their newfound experience. The singing was also often accompanied by arms raised in the air to express joy and adoration, and might well end with singing in tongues as people gave vent to their love for God.

There might even be a prophetic utterance. This could come from any member of the congregation and generally took one of three forms. It might be the quotation of a verse of Scripture which everyone then realised was peculiarly apt. It might be the description of a picture or vision that someone had experienced and felt impelled to share. It might be the expression of some word of challenge or encouragement which the speaker was sure came from the Holy Spirit. Of course, mistakes were sometimes made. But then the service moved on and the mistake was forgotten. The casual observer might also notice the extremely generous giving of these charismatics — one of the reasons why the bishops were not unhappy to have them in their diocese! Their giving, like their praises, was the outward expression of a profound, fresh, inner experience.

Spiritual gifts

Behind the scenes, however, other spiritual gifts were making themselves known. A common one was prayer for healing. I have been involved in this a number of times. A notable occasion was one in Wales where a group of us prayed for a man who was profoundly deaf. As we did so the phone in his home rang. He was, of course, astonished that he could hear it. He picked it up and he heard the voice of his son! On another occasion an Oxford student in our congregation had been in bed with a bad back for six weeks, had been X-rayed and was due to have an operation on his spine. He called together the leaders of the Christian group in his college and me, as the rector of his church, and we prayed for him. I sensed that God was present to heal, and asked him to get up. He did, went out and walked round the quad, and when he went back to the hospital his complete cure was confirmed. Such happenings seem to be occasional breakthroughs of God's Holy Spirit into our situation. Why they do not occur more often I do not know. That they happen at all gives me great joy.

Another unusual feature in the charismatic movement was the discernment of dark spiritual forces in a person, spoiling their life and bringing an unwelcome captivity to wild behaviour and oppressive addictions. It was found that a Christian who was full of the Holy Spirit could set people free from these unwelcome forces, just as in New Testament days. The whole idea is bizarre to Western minds, but anywhere in Asia, Africa or Latin America oppression by evil spirits is commonplace, and the attempt to remove them is what keeps witch doctors in business. I have personally (though reluctantly!) been involved in this 'deliverance ministry' of freeing people through the power of the Spirit, and know it to be real. But of course, as with the other gifts, it opens up the possibility of wrong diagnosis and grievous mistakes. The Church of England very wisely restricts this deliverance ministry to certain reliable persons with a proven track record in this very delicate area, operating under the authority of their bishop.

The leadership of David Watson

There were further notable expressions of this new movement. In some places, particularly York, where David Watson led the church of St Michael le Belfrey, families clubbed together to live in the same house and to provide hospitality for people around them in need. This of course saved rent, meant that only one washing machine was needed for the household, and enabled some of the members to be engaged in full-time Christian ministry while others held down regular jobs and the income was shared. This was a powerful witness to self-sacrifice and Christian fellowship, although in the long term it proved too utopian to last.

The most attractive embodiment of the charismatic movement was led by David and his team in York. The gifts and ministries mentioned above were all operative in his church, and attracted huge congregations. Soon David and his team were asked to lead services of renewal in major cathedrals up and down the land. They visited other countries, particularly Scandinavia and above all Ireland. Here they were effective in creating a community of Roman Catholic and Protestant charismatics spanning both sides of the Irish border during the troubles. They prayed with each other and by their sheer love minimised a great deal of the violence that would otherwise have broken out. David's ministry was cut short by cancer at the age of 50, and the Archbishop of Canterbury visited him before his death to express gratitude on behalf of the whole Church for the ministry he had given and the direction in which it had pointed.

But it is time to look more closely at the distinguishing marks of this remarkable movement of God's Spirit, which was not restricted to the seventies and eighties but whose impact can still be widely felt today

Characteristics of the charismatic movement

The name 'charismatic' is something of a misnomer. It has come to be applied to Christians who place particular emphasis on spiritual gifts such as tongues and prophecy. But the word derives from the Greek *charisma*, which means 'gracious gift'. The supreme 'charisma' of the Lord to us poor sinners is eternal life, as we are told in Romans 6:23. So in fact all true Christians are charismatics! But let's stay with the misnomer, so as to avoid confusion.

Tongues

The first characteristic that comes to most people's minds when charismatics are discussed is the gift of tongues. The New Testament has a good deal to say about this, particularly in 1 Corinthians 12 and 14, where it clearly means the pouring out of prayer or praise to God in 'vocables' or forms of speech or song that the intellect does not understand. It is primarily meant for private worship, but may be used in the congregation if there is someone who has been given by God the complementary gift of interpretation. To use this gift in public therefore requires great faith — that someone will be given the gift of interpretation! In contrast to the Pentecostal assertion that tongues is the initial proof of 'baptism in the Holy Spirit', charismatics, who are to be found in all denominations, rightly see it as just one of the gifts of the Spirit, which is given to some but not all Christians and is by no means necessarily an initiatory mark of spiritual awakening, let alone of spiritual maturity. They are right, because never in the New Testament is the phrase 'baptism "in" or "with" the Holy Spirit' used of a stage two initiation or 'second blessing'. On the contrary, the one baptism, being baptised or plunged into the realm of the Holy Spirit (coupled, of course, with repentance and faith), is what makes us Christians at all.

The phrase 'speaking in tongues' is actually unhelpful. It suggests the tongue lolling aimlessly in the mouth — and who wants that? It is rather a language of praise or prayer, given by the Spirit, and St Paul asserts it is designed to build us up. None of the gifts of the Spirit is a white elephant! A lot of the fuss about tongues is unnecessary. It is not the mark of high-octane initiation, it is not the reward for virtue, it is not the source of power. It is a sort of love language given by the Holy Spirit, and can be particularly helpful when you are cold in your prayers or do not know exactly what to pray for.

The renewing work of the Spirit

Once we see 'tongues' in proper proportion, the nature of the charismatic movement becomes clearer. It is simply a renewing of Christian life by the Holy Spirit of God. He is not a doctrine to be understood but a reality to be experienced. So it should not be surprising that God may not always use clergy for some particular ministry but may use any member of the congregation. After all, we are all 'members of one body'. It should not be surprising that the Holy Spirit may sometimes give to an ordinary church member some prophetic utterance, which may be predictive or may be much-needed encouragement for the benefit of all present. It should not be surprising that the Holy Spirit may sometimes bring healing when members of the church pray for a person in need. It should not be surprising that the Holy Spirit may exercise his divine power to release someone who is imprisoned by dark forces, and set them free from their addiction. Nor should we be surprised to find that the Holy Spirit may inspire the use of drama, dance and painting in church. Some or all of this may be encountered in churches that are vibrantly alive to the Holy Spirit. There is nothing spooky about it. It is plain New Testament Christianity. We only think it is over the top because our spiritual experience and expectation is so low. Perhaps the greatest characteristics of the charismatic movement are love for one another, a strong sense of gratitude and praise, an enhanced intensity in worship, and an expectancy that God will act.

Benefits of the charismatic movement

When God sees fit to make a movement like this spread worldwide we might expect to see some definite benefits. And so we can.

It has brought new life to countless churches, turning nominal churchpeople into vibrant believers, transforming worship and enabling worshippers to be full participants rather than observers.

It is a movement of deep faith in God, belief that with him all things are possible. It is a revolt against the straitjacket of Protestantism, confining the Spirit to an article in the creed, and of Catholicism, confining the Spirit to priests and sacraments. It is a revolt against the dead hand of theology that can write endless books about the Holy Spirit without ever suggesting that the authors know the power of the Spirit in their own lives. It can lay itself open to the danger of anti-intellectualism, or of overvaluing the more spectacular gifts. Sometimes those mistakes have certainly been made, but mercifully leaders have learnt fast.

It is very much a gospel movement. It has refused to remain content with the Catholic tendency to equate water baptism on its own with Christian initiation; or with the Protestant tendency to identify reception of the Spirit with a profession of conversion. It maintains that you can have these things without ever having received the life-giving Spirit of God into your very being. And that is a much-needed emphasis.

At its best the charismatic movement is fastidious in its pursuit of holiness, with every aspect of life surrendered to the Lord. Sometimes there have been spectacular lapses, especially by charismatics who persuaded themselves that sins of the flesh could not imperil their spiritual security. And sometimes this pursuit of holiness led to a particularly offensive arrogance among the so-called 'Spirit-filled' towards other Christians.

The charismatic movement is very much about belonging together in the body of Christ. It has made fellowship a reality for many who had never known its encouragement. Christians care for one another and are not embarrassed to express it in tears and laughter, concern in praying openly for one another, joy in dancing during worship, and a high degree of sacrificial service to the needy. The priesthood of all believers, so long assented to in theory, has become a reality. It is the very antithesis of the ministerial exclusivism which can afflict churches of all denominations. It aims to allow room for every member to play their God-given part.

In the ecumenical scene the charismatic movement has made spectacular gains. In the 1960s the World Council of Churches was grinding to a halt, failing to excite anyone and unable to discover more than a sentence on which all could agree. And then suddenly the charismatic movement came along, bringing deep and wonderful unity between Catholics, evangelicals, Baptists, Lutherans, the Orthodox and others. As one leader graphically explained it, the churches had operated like ducks in adjoining ponds with barriers separating them off. But when the rains came and the water level rose above the barriers, the ducks all mixed with abandon. That is what the charismatic movement at its best has done, and continues to do. Here again there are weaknesses, of course. One is the tendency to evade doctrine that might divide. Another is to cold-shoulder Christians who do not share the charismatic experience. But on the whole the charismatic movement has replaced a failing ecumenism and brought remarkable unity to Christians of different stripes.

Dangers in the charismatic movement

Whenever you get a very high tide, a load of rubbish can come in with it. And the charismatic high tide is no exception. Here are some of the dangers which charismatics have often fallen into, the flotsam and jetsam that have blemished the movement.

One is to use the 'baptism in the Spirit' language in a way which is not used in the New Testament and gives the painful impression that other Christians are not properly baptised.

Paul's letter to the Galatians shows up further problems. The charismatics in Galatia were always out for *more*, and Paul insisted that Christ and Christ alone was the blessing for Christians. Any doctrine that claims to add something to our sufficiency in Christ stands self-condemned.

Those charismatics in Galatia were always out for *power*, which fascinated them. It is the same in some circles today. Paul's reply is not to boast of his power but of his weakness, through which alone Christ's light can shine. He knew all about the marks of an apostle, in 'signs, wonders and miracles' as he puts it (2 Corinthians 12:12), but he preferred to use that power not to draw attention to himself but to endure the attacks that came his way in the course of his missionary work.

The charismatics in Galatia were also always out for *certainty*. That is why they, and some of their followers today, esteemed tongues and healings so highly. They are demonstrable evidence of God's reality. But Paul knows that we walk by faith, not by sight, and often God calls us to trust him in the dark, without any supporting evidence.

There have been other problems. Sometimes enthusiastic charismatics have been discourteous and dismissive to their pastors. Sometimes they have split to form another church, rather than waiting and praying for renewal in their own. Sometimes they have displayed an arrogance very alien to the spirit of Jesus, behaving as though their possession of some gift was due to their own achievements and not to divine generosity. Alas, the movement, though rich in blessing, has not lacked failings.

The Toronto Blessing

Perhaps the most notorious cause for concern has been the so-called 'Toronto Blessing'. This came to prominence in the mid-nineties when a small Vineyard church on the edge of Toronto Airport suddenly drew thousands a night for a seven-day-a-week ministry of praise, teaching and charismatic phenomena such as shaking, falling to the ground, weeping, laughter and 'revelations'. Most of these phenomena can be found in the Scriptures, and they are fully documented in past revivals such as that under John Wesley in England and Jonathan Edwards in the US. But there were extravagances, too, such as barking like a dog, and these led to a lot of negative publicity. This movement greatly intrigued charismatic churches in Britain, and planeloads of Christians went to Toronto to visit. Indeed, for several years people flocked there from all over the world to see what was going on and to join in the experience. I visited the church when I was lecturing to a postgraduate class in Toronto on the subject of the Holy

Spirit, and though the students were very surprised, they were also impressed by the atmosphere of love and the tremendous self-sacrifice of the regular congregation, who graciously hosted thousands night after night. There were some four thousand there the night our class went. The teaching was not particularly brilliant, but it was not bizarre. There is no doubt that there was an expectation that many would be 'slain in the Spirit', i.e. become unconscious and fall to the ground. There were markings on the floor to ensure that this happened in an orderly fashion! I can assure you that nobody got pushed, and I have several times myself experienced that sinking to the ground under the Holy Spirit's gentle touch. I fancy it is God's anaesthetic as he does something deep inside us. Often when people got up they were full of joy. Sometimes they knew what had happened to them and why it was needed. At other times they were aware of nothing except a profound rejoicing in God's love for them. That sense of love is a lasting impression in my memory about the strange happenings at Toronto. What is not so widely known is that many thousands of clergy received ministry during the daytime, and went back to their churches with the flame of love to God reignited.

What is the value of the so-called Toronto Blessing? That is the important question. As the Archbishop of York once said to me when we were discussing all this, 'I don't mind them falling down. I want to know if they are any good when they get up!' That says it all.

The truth seems to be that a great many of them are some good when they get up. A prevailing sense of joy, a deepened love for Jesus and a substantial measure of healing and reconciliation seem to be associated with this 'Toronto' experience. Many people discern a fresh area of service, some lapsed people come back to the church, and some who come to enquire or scoff are converted. The church members at Toronto are not at all legalistic. They are not interested in making money. They do not lionise their leadership. They are very generous to the streams of visitors who fly in from all over the world. However, the quality of teaching is often weak. Emphasis on the Spirit to such a degree can detract from the power of God's revelation in Scripture: the Spirit and the Word belong together in God's economy. The sacraments do not figure highly. A sniff of spiritual pride and self-absorption has been noticed among some members of the church. Many of the locals go along several times a week for a spiritual 'fix', which is not healthy. And of course there have been some crazy things like growling and roaring while attributing that to the Holy Spirit. Perhaps that is a reminder that careful pastoral care, shrewd discernment, firm leadership, biblical norms and wise counsel are essential requisites when spiritual gifts are allowed free rein.

New expressions

There is much more that could be said. John Wimber, with his exceptional spiritual insight ('gift of knowledge'), had an enormous influence in Britain, not least through his partnership with David Watson in St Michael's, York. Whole new denominations like Pioneer, New Frontiers and Vineyard sprang from the charismatic movement, when the new wine of the movement could not be contained in the old wineskins of the established church. Cell churches began to multiply, all springing from the same source. The Alpha course, centred in Holy Trinity Brompton, has now spread all over the world and has led hundreds of thousands to Christ, as has a similar course, Christianity Explored. New styles in worship, the New Wine celebrations, church planting and the emergence of new forms of church among young people, sportsmen, actors and others — all this is part of the astonishing overflowing of the banks when the river of the Holy Spirit rose high in the middle of the twentieth century. And, thankfully, the effects remain. This is not like some revivals which have speedily run into the sand, as the Welsh revival did. It continues to affect the life of all the churches in some way or other. It may not be as dynamic now as when it began, but it has proved pervasive and lasting.

What do we owe to the charismatic movement?

Dr J. I. Packer, a distinguished Anglican not closely associated with the charismatic movement, gave this assessment of its value in his book *Keep in Step with the Spirit* (p. 196).

1 Rediscovery of the living God and his Christ, and the supernatural dimensions of Christian living, through Spirit baptism or the Spirit's 'release'.
2 Returning to the Bible as the inspired Word of God, to nourish one's soul upon it.
3 Habits of public and private devotion designed to bring the whole person, body and soul, into total, expectant, dependence on the Holy Spirit (glossolalia comes in here).
4 A leisurely, participatory style of public praise and prayer.
5 A use of spiritual gifts for ministry in the Body of Christ.
6 Exploration of the possibilities of ministry through a communal lifestyle.
7 An active commitment by this and other means to reach out to the needy in evangelism and service.
8 A high level of expectancy that the hand of God will again and again be shown in striking providences ('miracles'), prophetic messages to this or that person, visions, supernatural healings, and similar manifestations.

These are massive blessings that God has showered upon us in our lifetime. They are a graphic reminder that however great the interventions God has made in the past, at times of need in his Church he can break in again. If I were to give an assessment of the value of this movement I would want to draw attention to the challenges it has offered to the established way in which we operated. It challenged the institutionalism of the Church. It challenged its dry intellectualism. It challenged one-person leadership. It challenged unbelief. And the missionary passion to which it has given rise challenged the introversion of the Church.

For all this we can thank God and take courage.

8

Rivers in the east
Mongolia and Singapore

We have looked at a number of occasions in
Britain when God has broken into a particularly
bleak period in the Church's life. In the next two chapters we shall look at examples of utterly unexpected
divine intervention on the other side of the globe, in
the Far East, in countries where the church was so small
as to be negligible.

There are many places that one might choose.
Cambodia, for instance, is a land where the 'Killing
Fields' of the Khmer Rouge have turned into the 'Living
Fields' today. Fifty years of nearly fruitless toil followed
the 1920s, when the gospel was first planted among the
rice farmers in the north. Then between 1975 and 1979
Pol Pot and his Khmer Rouge slaughtered at least two
million of the seven million Cambodian population,
including almost the entire church. Thousands of starv-
ing Cambodians streamed into refugee camps in
Thailand and elsewhere, where there was an amazing
spiritual movement in the 1970s, a counterpart to the
indescribable slaughter of those years in their own

country. And now the camps are closed, the refugees have returned, the chief exterminator Comrade Dutch has been converted and is a Christian preacher, and a flourishing church of more than twenty thousand is free and growing throughout the country. That story has been poignantly told by Don Cormack, for twenty years a missionary in Cambodia, in his acclaimed book *Killing Fields, Living Fields*.

Wonderful as the movement in Cambodia is, I shall not pursue it here. Instead I have decided to turn to two very different places, rural Mongolia and urban Singapore, and examine the revivals that have taken place there in recent years. I will reserve the biggest and most astounding story of them all, the awakening in China, for the next chapter. First, Mongolia.

Mongolia

Recent history

Mongolia is a land-locked country twelve times the size of England but with a population of only just over three million. It lies between Russia in the north and China in the south. Its people have been largely nomadic since prehistoric times. Over the centuries the country has been part of a variety of empires, but at times Mongolia has been in the ascendant, particularly in the thirteenth century under Ghengis Khan, who carved out one of the largest land empires in history, from the Pacific to Afghanistan, from Russia to Germany. His grandson Kublai Khan went on to conquer China! But that did not last long. Mongolia shrank to its previous borders, and in the sixteenth and seventeenth centuries fell strongly under the influence of Tibetan Buddhism. By the nineteenth century Mongolia formed part of the Chinese empire.

But in 1911 the ruling Qing Dynasty collapsed, and Mongolia declared independence. There followed a confused period of struggle between Russia and China to possess the country. This culminated in 1924 in the formation of Mongolia as only the second independent Socialist country in the world, in effect a satellite of Russia. It stayed firmly under Russian influence for most of the twentieth century.

In 1989 the Berlin Wall fell, and the Soviet empire began to disintegrate. This profoundly affected Mongolia. There were hunger strikes and riots in the main square of the capital. The communist-oriented government resigned en bloc, a new constitution was put in place and democratic elections were held in what then became a parliamentary democratic republic. Somewhat dazed by it all, society made a new start. Windows were opened towards the wider world, including the West. And freedoms emerged, hitherto unknown — among them freedom of religion.

Religious history

The religious scene was somewhat complicated. The nomadic tribes had usually practised animism, with shamans purporting to control access to the spirit world. But the planting of more than seven hundred Tibetan Buddhist monasteries in the country during the sixteenth and seventeenth centuries had been successful in making the country almost wholly Buddhist – a Buddhism, however, that was heavily tinged with the preceding animism. This suffered a sharp reverse in the 1930s, when under Russian influence the monasteries were dissolved and the monks dispersed or shot. Atheism became dominant.

However, when the new Republic was formed in the 1990s with freedom of religion, atheism lost much of its influence. They had experienced it, and it had failed to deliver. It was succeeded by a great openness and desire to explore. Of course, some people remained atheist, and there was a substantial revival of Buddhism, but many folk began to investigate fresh spiritual routes. One of those new routes was Christianity.

The opportunity was enormous. The country had no recent history of missions, no Western colonial history, no established church, no recognisable Christians and no Bible! It was a clean slate.

The Christian gospel had not always been unknown in Mongolia. The country had been influenced in the sixth century by Nestorian Christianity, which held that Jesus embodied two separate personalities, human and divine. Down the years it had boasted several queens who were Christians, including the mother of Kublai Khan. Astonishingly, Kublai wrote to the Pope asking for a hundred missionaries to come and preach in Mongolia. The Pope sent only two Dominican friars, who turned back before they reached the country. Christianity might well have become the predominant faith of Mongolia eight hundred years ago! One of the greatest missionary opportunities in history had gone begging, and Mongolia turned to Tibetan Buddhism. In more recent times the Christian faith, nourished by intrepid missionaries like 'the Trio', Mildred Cable and Eva and Francesca French in the 1920s, was ruthlessly extinguished after seven decades of Russian communist influence. There were no known Christians in the country when, in 1992, a handful of missionaries from Finland, the US and especially Korea arrived in Mongolia.

Christian revival

These newcomers came at a time of turbulent social revolution, and were plunged into the social instability and unrest that followed the collapse of the communist planned economy. Within the next fifteen years they witnessed the growth of a church from nothing to more than forty thousand members!

There were some similarities with the Acts of the Apostles in this astonishing explosion of faith. For instance, when people heard the gospel for the first time they tended to disappear. Where had they gone? To tell their relatives and friends in other villages! The main work of evangelism was not done by the missionaries from abroad, but by the indigenous population once they had been fired by the good news of Christ. There was some preaching in the streets, and a great deal of visiting from house to house. Perhaps the two key instruments during this astonishing period of advance were the highly accessible New Testament and the *Jesus* film, a product of Campus Crusade, which has been dubbed in countless languages and shown all over the world.

How did the revival come about?

The revival was enormously assisted by the emergence of an idiomatic Mongolian translation of the Scriptures, so crucial for the nurture of new believers and the establishment of the church. An Englishman had set about translating the New Testament into Mongolian back in the 1970s, and it came off the press at the very time it was needed, when the gospel arrived back in the country and the first believers came to faith in 1992.

Of course there was opposition. This came primarily from within the families of the converts, whether atheist or Buddhist. Christian children could have a tough time in their schools. In the countryside opposition could be instigated by the provincial authorities if they were so disposed. But as people gradually began to see the quality of the lives of the Christians and their practical service to the community, opposition greatly diminished. Overseas missionaries were rarely troubled by officialdom so long as they kept strictly within the terms of their visas.

The question remains, how did this movement grow to such an extent that the Christian population moved from zero to more than forty thousand between 1992 and the census of 2008? That is phenomenal growth, and it is continuing. What accounts for it?

As always in such times of revival, the architect is God. Mongolia's time had come, and Christians could only stand back in awe and rejoice at this rebirth of the faith which had enjoyed some influence during past periods of Mongolian history but had subsequently been entirely extinguished. However, there were several human elements from which we can learn.

One was the fact that this young church had never fallen for the heresy that Christianity was for their private benefit. They knew it must be passed on. Evangelism was natural to them: it was in their DNA.

Another was the focus on church planting. An outstanding Korean, Pastor Hwang, was a key figure in planting churches out of the capital, Ulaanbaatar, where he worked. He had an eye, like the apostle Paul, for strategically planting little groups of believers in the capital city of each province. But he was by no means an exception. Hugh Kemp, himself a missionary in Mongolia and author of a major book, *Steppe by Step*, mentions that the church with which he was involved planted nineteen daughter churches before its own sixth birthday in November 1998. Some of the growth came from short outreaches into the countryside in an old Russian van, encouraging any believers they found and explaining the gospel to all who would listen. Some of the growth started from tiny initiatives. One young man took an eight-hour bus journey to the south Gobi and began chatting to youths who were hanging around the sports stadium. They threw stones at him, but he persevered and in due course a small church came into being. Ten years later he was speaking at the anniversary of that church to a crowd of three thousand people in that same stadium, drawn from fifteen or so small but growing churches across the province. Nowadays those very churches are mainly responsible for evangelism, and it takes place as unbelievers notice the lives of believers and are attracted to the message of the local churches, which are now to be found in every province of the land.

Another crucial factor in the rapid growth of the church was, as we have seen, the provision in 1990 of a colloquial Mongol version of the New Testament. Happily, most people in the country could read. Here was something new, and, along with the *Jesus* film it drew a great deal of interest, in the new spirit of openness at the start of the Republic. Of course, the Bible and prayer always figure large in the growth of these churches. Corporate prayer is central, particularly on Fridays in the Korean-led churches where everyone prays out loud at once.

A further important factor in the expansion of the church is the attention given to nurture. Whereas many Western churches have little effective nurture in place, this is not so in Mongolia. Lots of the churches use two short introductory courses, one on the Bible and the other on Christian basics until the newcomers (nomadic by instinct!) have got used to a habit of regular attendance. Then two of the courses used in many parts of the developing world come into play, Abundant Light and Abundant Life. The former is concerned to give a broad overview of the Bible, the latter helps with living as a Christian in the workplace. Other churches use what they call G12, consisting of small groups where the leader has extensive training materials to help the twelve people for whom he or she is responsible. One way and another, great attention is paid to nurture.

Leadership

Leadership is another area essential for growth, and is given a high priority. Since Mongolians are proving very capable at evangelising their own country, missionaries find their place in training and equipping pastors and church planters. Training for home group leaders and Sunday school teachers is generally done in the local church, but there are now various more advanced training institutions, such as the Bible Training Centre. Distance learning is provided by the Mongolian Centre for Theological Education by Extension. Some of the ablest young Christians study abroad. As I write, there is a Mongolian doing a doctorate in theology at Oxford!

The churches are to a large extent independent, and although there is some degree of shared leadership normally one pastor does the teaching. Some of these pastors simply emerge from the congregations and assume leadership naturally, but there is a distinct difference between these unordained church leaders and the authorised pastors, who have had Bible college training and are recognised by the wider Mongolian church. When the Bible College began, it was used for short intensive bursts, designed to help those who could come in for limited periods. Now it caters for full-time students, and it is no longer the only one. For instance, the Assemblies of God run their own Bible college. Does your heart sink at this point, fearing that the denominationalism exported from the West could spoil this beautiful work of God? No, that is not the case. Although the Lutherans, Baptists and Presbyterians have affiliation worldwide, their mutual relationships remain very close in Mongolia. The churches run city-wide evangelistic campaigns together, joint Easter and Christmas celebrations, shared theological education, various development projects, and cooperation with the government on a variety of social issues.

New hope

I pressed my missionary friend Graham Aylett to know what, in his opinion, accounted for the meteoric growth of this church from nothing to many thousands in just a few years in such an unlikely part of the world, remote as it was from Christian influences. He acknowledged the sociological factors such as the huge social upheaval in the early 1990s which facilitated the proclamation of the gospel. The controlling ideology of communism had crumbled, and people were wondering where their hopes could be anchored. Many people told him, 'Coming to Christ has given me new hope.' But he had no doubt that the intrinsic power of the message has been of more importance than the external factors. Fear of the spirits, fear of death, which had crippled the people for generations under both communism and Buddhism, was banished in the light of a Saviour who had risen from the dead. A new sense of purpose gets these new believers out of bed in the morning: 'Jesus has given me a reason for living' was how one of them described it. They believe God has a plan for their nation and they have a place in it. They have a hope which reaches beyond death. They are confident that because of the cross their sins are dealt with. These things, basic to Christianity, lie at the heart of the extraordinary spread of the gospel in Mongolia.

Strengths and weaknesses

What are the strengths and weaknesses of this young church? The weakness is perhaps the lure of materialism. The country is rich in minerals and these are now energetically being developed. There is the temptation of a prosperity gospel which on the one hand flatters those who succeed, but on the other hand breeds discouragement for those who see no material improvement in their circumstances and wonder if God does not care for them. These temptations are familiar in the West as well. But what is less familiar is the strength demonstrated by this young Mongolian church. They have a clear vision: to see 10 per cent of their nation won for Christ within the next seven years. They see this as a new goal for their landlocked country. They are buoyed up by hope, confident of their relationship with God. Heaven and hell are very real for them. They believe that people are lost without the gospel, and are determined to reach as many of them as possible with the message that has transformed their own lives. Had these convictions marked the church in Europe, our present low level of spirituality might have been very different.

Singapore

It would be hard to find a greater contrast than between the sparsely populated nomadic country of Mongolia and the intensely urban and industrial island of Singapore. But an amazing outbreak of spiritual renewal has erupted there in recent years, which is both encouraging and instructive.

Singapore has much in common with the West. It is a highly educated, multicultural, industrial, English-speaking society. It has only been independent of Britain since 1963, and since then has prospered exponentially. The existing spiritual life in the small Anglican churches had been unimpressive. But in the 1970s a major revival began to emerge, primarily based in Singapore's Anglican cathedral, and has spread to the other three dioceses in the Province of Southeast Asia, namely West Malaysia, Sabah and Kuching. As I have had the privilege of being quite heavily involved with the Province, much of what follows comes from my own personal experience and observation.

The transformation of the Bishop of Singapore

There were several streams which combined to create this river of revival. The first was the appointment of an indigenous bishop, Chiu Ban It, in 1966. He had four main goals: the development of prayer, evangelism, witness and service. By the time he stood down in 1982 he had seen each of them partially fulfilled. He laid great emphasis on the Bible, he concentrated on young people (54 per cent of the population being under twenty-one) and he broke down denominational barriers. But perhaps the greatest factor was the renewal of the bishop himself.

In the early 1970s the worldwide charismatic movement reached Singapore and caused considerable confusion. Bishop Chiu was highly suspicious of the prayer in tongues, the prayers for healing, the prophetic utterances and the vibrant forms of worship. This all seemed so un-Anglican in a highly traditionalist cathedral that used sixteenth-century plainsong in its Eucharist. But the new enthusiasm spread fast, and 'charismatic' churches sprang up within the Anglican diocese. This was not at all to the liking of the bishop. Not, that is, until in 1972 he attended a World Council of Churches conference in Bangkok on the subject of salvation and stumbled across a book that challenged him to ask God to break into his life afresh. So he cried to God to do just that.

'God was suddenly very close,' he said.

My heart was filled with life, joy and peace instead of anger, despair and gloom. The dam of the mind burst, and I found myself uttering new sounds and syllables which had no meaning to my mind but which I knew in my spirit were fluently giving expression to the praise welling up within me.

This experience revolutionised the bishop's ministry. The next year he invited an overseas charismatic, Edgar Webb, to lead healing sessions in the cathedral, and asked me to speak at the Friday night prayer service. I was astonished that anyone would come to a weeknight prayer meeting, judging by the rigid formalism I had seen in a previous visit. But the cathedral was packed. I was asked to preach evangelistically, and there was substantial response. The bishop then gave an additional sermon on healing, and invited people to come to the Communion rail. I was amazed to see physical healings of an incontrovertible nature – I think of a man throwing away his crutches and another whose hearing was restored. And it was that night that I myself received the gift of tongues!

The fires of revival

But this was only the beginning. The diocese began to blaze with the fire of the Holy Spirit. New churches emerged, and there was one of those spontaneous spiritual advances that nobody can organise but everybody notices when it happens. The cathedral itself became the centre of all this activity. Charismatic praise and prayer meetings took place weekly, as did seminars on the work of the Holy Spirit, which continued for seven years and had a massive influence among Christians of various denominations.

Canon James Wong, one of the key figures in the revival, wrote:

These healing services marked a turning point for the Anglican Church in Singapore, and introduced a new dimension of power and life in the Spirit to the Church. Instead of being an inward looking institution the Anglican Church began to reach out to the lost, the sick and needy. The gospel came alive in the church. Signs and wonders accompanied the preaching of the gospel. This kind of power-evangelism became the church's priority.

Criteria of authentic spirituality

Needless to say, the renewal movement was not welcomed by every section of the church. They objected, with good reason, to the various extravagances that appeared at the start of the revival, such as instances of excessive noise, divisive tendencies, spiritual pride and exaggerated claims. So the bishop, while now welcoming the renewal, laid down shrewd criteria of authenticity. He encouraged seven questions that should be asked of any phenomenon claiming to come from the Holy Spirit.

Is it consistent with Holy Scripture?
Is it motivated by 'agape' love?
Is it for the common good?
Is it accompanied by the fruit of the Spirit?
Does it guide into truth?

Does it glorify Jesus?

Does the spirit behind it, when tested, affirm that Jesus is the incarnate Son of God?

Wise advice. For the charismatic movement can be chaotic unless it is based on a strong biblical foundation and kept within a firm church framework.

Handing over to Bishop Moses Tay

I personally witnessed the transformation of Bishop Chiu from a weak leader, afraid of his clergy and dependent on psychological counselling, to a marvellous example of God's power made perfect in weakness. He himself told me the secret:

The Lord made it very clear to me that he wanted his Church back. The Diocese of Singapore was not mine with him helping, but his with me helping! When I humbly submitted to him he began to do great things in the Diocese and Church of Singapore.

This new humility, which came from his being filled by the Holy Spirit, led to an extraordinary revitalising in the Anglican Church in Singapore, and was a powerful demonstration to me of the nature of true Christian leadership. By the time he retired in 1982 the fire was lit and all was ready for major advance along the path he had pioneered. All that was needed was a strong

Spirit-filled leader. And God led the diocese to choose one, in the person of the Revd Dr Moses Tay.

Chiu Ban It had a remarkable vision while he was in office. He saw a well, overgrown with weeds and holding little water. When he asked God what he should do about it, the reply was that the drought is a good time to clear out the well, for when the rains come the well will not be able to contain all the water. Yet the bishop himself was not to be the one to refill the well. That would be the task of someone else.

And so it proved. The Revd Dr Moses Tay, a gifted hospital superintendent and non-stipendiary minister, ordained only four years earlier, was elected bishop. He soon showed what he was made of. He built on the foundations Ban It had left him, but his clear-headedness, mental toughness and organisational ability, coupled with his deep experience of the Holy Spirit, marked him out as exceptional. It was no surprise that he became the first archbishop when the new Province of South East Asia was formed in 1996. I believe he contributed four main elements to the revival.

Four major strands in the revival of the Province

The first was his emphasis on leadership. Singapore soon became a byword for training ordained and lay leaders for the church. He was more concerned to have godly clergy, full of the Holy Spirit, even if they had not gone to theological college, than less committed men who had gone through the recognised ordination training. His controversial ordination of those he thought suitable may well have been right for the circumstances, but it was not appreciated by Singapore's Trinity Theological College! However, it was his lay training that led to the remarkable strength of the church. His plan was threefold. The first part led enquirers through conversion and initial nurture to confirmation and a systematic plan for reading the New Testament. Every church member was encouraged to go through the programme, and the vast majority did. This, of course, produced large numbers of well-taught laypeople, enthusiastic to move on to the second phase. The second phase focused on equipping lay Christians for different aspects of ministry, based on the premise that all Christians, not some, are called to be ministers of Christ. This wide-ranging diocesan lay training programme, first introduced in conjunction with the diocesan mission in 1984, was conducted at the parish level, but overseen by the diocese. The third tier in training was an ambitious programme embracing biblical studies, church growth, evangelism and discipleship which led to the Certificate in Church Ministry. I doubt if there is anywhere in the world a training programme among church members which compares with this in biblical knowledge, practical skills and evangelistic and pastoral concern.

Not content with building up the church, Moses Tay had a passion for expanding it. He did this in three ways.

The first was by occasional large missions and celebrations. He even hosted an Anglican Congress on World Evangelisation in 1990. I was there. It was superb, although largely ignored by Western churchmen.

The second was by encouraging cell groups, an initiative begun under Bishop Chiu. These were small home meetings which fostered fellowship among the members and reached out to the people in their neighbourhood. Designed to supplement rather than supplant the regular Sunday worship, they proved extremely valuable. They cut down on backsliding, nurtured leadership skills, were a natural vehicle for informal evangelism, and alerted members to social needs around them. They were also ideal at building up young Christians and providing a support base for missionary ventures in other countries. These cells, now transdenominational, have continued in Singapore and are to be found in almost every street of the island.

Archbishop Tay's third initiative was breathtaking. He refused to allow the passion for evangelism, which characterised his episcopate, to be confined to the island of Singapore. He was so concerned to reach the 350 million unevangelised members of nearby nations that he appointed some of his senior clergy as 'deans' of adjoining countries (where as yet there were no Anglicans). Thus James Wong became Dean of Indonesia, Gerald Khoo of Thailand, Norman Beale of Nepal. They were all commissioned to get visitor's visas and start an Anglican work from scratch. The converts were brought to Singapore for training and some of them, in due course, for ordination. Who ever heard of such a thing in the West? We have much to learn from these intrepid Singaporeans.

If concentration on leadership and mission were two of Tay's strengths, a third was community involvement. These Singaporeans were no 'happy clappy' self-absorbed believers, but dedicated to meeting the physical needs all around them. They have concentrated on education, providing schools, kindergartens and childcare centres. Their medical work is extensive. They run hospitals, centres for the emotionally and mentally disturbed, and an extensive counselling network which is enormously appreciated.

But these Singaporean Christians go further still. They make a territorial commitment to their community, aiming not so much to fill their churches but to win the community for its rightful Lord. Churches take responsibility for the area surrounding them, and offer street parties, computer training, food distribution and the meeting of need in countless ways. This is no mere social service. It is all an outworking of their deep devotion to Christ. 'Serving the community is a major objective,' wrote Moses Tay. 'We do this as an expression of God's love. By participating in community service the church becomes relevant to the community.' Thus when they ran an island-wide campaign 'Love Singapore', it rang true. That was what the church stood for.

Anyone who knows Moses Tay appreciates that he is a man of profound conviction. If you can persuade him that some course of action is biblical he will follow it, whatever the cost. If he is being urged to action which is not in accordance with the Bible he will eschew it, whatever the cost. This is what lies behind his famed conservatism. He is not conservative in practice — actually, he is extremely imaginative and inventive, prepared to take great risks for God. But he is conservative about Scripture. He is faithful to his vows made both as a priest and as a bishop to teach and live by the Christianity revealed in Scripture. No Anglicans are ordained unless they can answer affirmatively questions such as 'Do you accept the Holy Scriptures as revealing all things necessary for salvation through faith in Christ?' and 'Will you uphold the truth of the gospel against error?' The sad thing is that many clergy in the West make this profession but do not believe it and do not act on it. Nobody could say that of Moses Tay. He knows the power of Scripture to shape a church and to convert unbelievers. He sticks fearlessly to its teachings. As a result, many of a more liberal persuasion regard him as awkward and controversial. He was so regarded in successive Lambeth Conferences. But that is unfair. In lifestyle he is modest, in language courteous, in attitude non-aggressive, in self-assessment humble. But when other bishops are flagrantly opposing the teaching of the Bible, he is as fearless as a lion. And he has instilled this strong biblical stance into the very lifeblood of the renewal in Singapore. That is one of the keys to the continuing renewal in that remarkable island state, and along with his social concern, his evangelism and his leadership training, it is a major element in his legacy. There is much for the worldwide Church to learn from Singapore.

9

Floodtide
Revival in China

Nothing like it has been seen in living memory —
perhaps never in the history of the Church.
Christianity reached China in the seventh century, but
did not at that time become a significant feature in the
life of the nation. Despite a fair amount of mission
work in China over the succeeding centuries, the most
populous nation in the world turned its back on
Christianity under Mao Zedong, the founding father of
the People's Republic of China. He purported to be 'the
living god' and brooked no competition. All missionaries had been ejected in 1952, and the Christian faith
was already under considerable pressure when
Chairman Mao, stung by the disintegration of much of
his Great Leap Forward, launched the Cultural
Revolution in 1966 and began a systematic and ruthless
attack on the church. He died in 1976, with the church
effectively eliminated from Chinese society — or at
least driven completely underground.

Mao's chosen successor was Hua Guofeng, but he
was gradually out-manoeuvred by Deng Xiaoping.

Once exiled by Mao, Deng now became the de facto leader of the country and set out to reverse the devastation left by the Cultural Revolution. He changed many of its policies and adopted a more moderate 'open door' approach, often known as the 'Beijing Spring'. In 1979, when he began to gain full control of the country, there were still no churches officially open anywhere in China. But that year proved to be critical for the launch of the Christian advance. Now, there are more than fifty-seven thousand Protestant churches, reopened with government permission, as well as some forty thousand registered 'meeting points', and vast numbers of 'underground' churches that are unregistered.

As for the number of Christians in the country, accurate figures are impossible to discover. The lowest estimate is forty million, the largest a hundred and twenty million. At a recent academic conference in Oxford of high-powered Chinese, some of them Christian and some not, I was told that there are about eighteen million in the official Three Self churches, about fifty or sixty million in the unregistered 'house churches', and about twelve million Roman Catholics. These are, no doubt, broad estimates, but on any showing this is miraculous growth, recognised with chagrin in communist official documents. The government is alarmed because in several parts of China more people are joining the church than the Communist Party, and they are powerless to stop it.

Before we set out to examine this astonishing phenomenon, we need to be clear that, although there had been efforts to introduce Christianity into China over the centuries, these were largely confined to the coast. They had proved to be fairly ineffective before the middle of the nineteenth century, when Hudson Taylor and his colleagues formed the China Inland Mission (CIM) in 1865. In February 1866 George Stott, a Scottish CIM missionary with a wooden leg, arrived in China and settled in Wenzhou. This was a prosperous port in Zhejiang province in the southeast of the country. There was not a single Christian there. In due course a small church emerged. One of the Chinese boys who became a Christian was severely disabled, paralysed down one side. But he became the first native Chinese evangelist in the area. The gospel spread quite rapidly, survived seven decades of hardship, and was only extinguished in the late 1960s as Mao with his militantly atheistic Red Guards virtually ravaged the Chinese church. Pastors were sent to labour camps, churches were closed, Bibles burnt, and the area was named an 'atheistic zone' where every effort was made to erase the very thought of God. For more than two decades the church in Wenzhou seemed to have disappeared.

However, under Deng's economic and cultural reforms, the area began to flourish. So did the church! The old CIM church building in the city centre was reopened in 1979 after the collapse of the Cultural Revolution, and was soon packed with a thousand worshippers. Today this erstwhile 'atheist zone' is known as 'Jerusalem in China' with some six hundred thousand evangelical Protestants — 10 per cent of the population of Wenzhou! Nowadays 'greater Wenzhou' has over a thousand churches officially open for worship, and a similar number of 'meeting points'. Indeed, in the rural areas around this great port there is a church almost every kilometre, and in Yongjiao, one of the counties in the province, there are 130,000 registered Christian adults out of a population of 730,000: that is to say, some 18 per cent. The one-legged Scotsman and the paralysed Chinese evangelist would be delighted to see that the seeds they planted in the latter part of the nineteenth century had grown into such a mighty forest towards the end of the twentieth!

If we travel from the southeast to the northwest, much the same story emerges. The city of Lanzhou is capital of the arid northwestern 'panhandle' province of Gansu, stretching alongside the Great Wall. Thousands of baptisms are taking place there every year. The facts are recorded in detail in the massive two-volume *The Shaping of Modern China* by A. J. Broomhall; and Tony Lambert, former British diplomat in Beijing and now director of China Research for OMF International, gives the most accessible overview of the revival in his book *China's Christian Millions*. He tells how in 1990 he walked into the old church of Lanzhou, built a hundred years earlier by the China Inland Mission, and witnessed two hundred and fifty baptisms, conducted by two old pastors standing for hours up to their waist in water. Lanzhou has at least twenty thousand Christians meeting in eight registered churches and thirty-nine smaller venues. This gives some idea of the extent and spread of Christianity in modern-day China. The official registered church records half a million adult baptisms a year, and unregistered churches baptise far more.

Before we investigate the Chinese church situation further, we must note a crucial distinction, between churches that are recognised by the state and those that are not. In 1979 China officially recognised five 'patriotic' religions — Buddhism, Taoism, Islam, Catholicism and Protestantism — where religious activity was allowed under strict conditions.

The Three Self Church

The Three Self Patriotic Movement is recognised by the government as the Protestant branch of Christianity. It is self-governing, self-financing and self-propagating, and must be loyal to the Party, which thus actually controls the Church. The government determines who can join the church (no soldiers, no Communist Party officials, no teachers, nobody under eighteen) and what it can teach (nothing about the resurrection or the second coming, nothing against abortion or communism). They are forbidden to operate outside the registered church buildings and meeting points.

It would be easy to be somewhat sceptical about the Three Self Church, labouring as it does under such massive restrictions. It is often infiltrated by government spies, and some of its leadership have a suspect past history. However, it would be a mistake to write off the Three Self Church. Not only are there vast numbers of these official churches in the country, but nobody can deny their zeal, evangelism and godly behaviour. They persist and grow in spite of the manifold difficulties they face. In some provinces there is continued persecution by the authorities. Elsewhere there is a pathetic shortage of pastors and Bibles, and so they suffer an enormous handicap. Since they are not allowed to evangelise or baptise anyone under eighteen, they are unable to engage in any youth and children's work, the lifeblood of so much Christianity elsewhere in the world. They operate with a mixture of courage and caution, taking care not to upset the authorities unnecessarily but increasingly passionate about evangelism and nurture. One registered pastor smilingly related that he baptised many people openly in church, and then went out and baptised many more at night in the streams secretly, because the Three Self Church is prohibited from operating outside its premises!

Increasingly the authorities are recognising the good that Christians do. They set up medical clinics, repair roads and bridges, and give generous support when some natural disaster strikes. Whereas in the days of Mao Christians were a despised and suspect minority, now they are often seen as model citizens. In 2007 the Communist Party added an amendment to its constitution, urging its members to 'rally religious believers in making contribution to economic and social development'.

There is a great deal of corruption in Chinese society at large, and the government is reluctantly forced to employ and promote Christians because they are generally impervious to bribes. But recognition is patchy and in some parts of the country official persecution continues. Whether persecuted or not, churches do not find it easy to train their leaders. There is only one national theological seminary, and competition for places in the few provincial ones is keen − often fifty applicants are turned away for every available place. Its buildings are in dire need of repair, the library bereft of modern books and the accommodation spartan. However, the distinguished Professor Wu has made a huge difference. He survived many years in a labour camp, and returned to train young students and write books for them − since his library had been destroyed in the Cultural Revolution. Although more than twenty million Bibles have now been printed in China since 1979, they are nothing like sufficient to meet demand, and the hunger for other Christian literature goes largely unmet. The government permits registered Christian organisations, but it certainly does not make life easy for them.

House churches

The other main constituent in the revival is the house church movement. This is quite distinct from the Three Self Church, though there is often considerable rapport between them. They are called 'house churches' because they are not allowed to own church property and consequently meet in houses. They are not legally recognised because they have declined to come forward and be registered with the government. There are several reasons for this resistance on their part. One is that they insist that Christ, not the Communist Party, is the head of the Church. Another is that they are not prepared to put up with the restrictions placed upon the Three Self Church. And third, they are suspicious of the integrity of the Three Self Church because of its history of compromise and collusion with the government. They are prepared to go it alone and risk the consequences. Some Western Christians, misled by lack of information and deliberate disinformation put out by the Chinese authorities and even by the Three Self Church, regard the house churches as extremist sects who provoke the authorities and deserve the punishment they get. Doubtless there are extravagances and heretical tendencies in some of these underground churches where the leadership is often very young and untaught. But essentially these are evangelical churches, strong on Scripture, passionate in evangelism. They are composed of loyal Chinese citizens who are not prepared to accept state control. Like the apostle Peter before the Sanhedrin, they believe 'we must obey God rather than men'.

The term 'house church' is somewhat confusing. In the West it is usually applied to charismatic groups of churches that have split off from mainline denominations. But these Chinese house churches have not split from anywhere and are not necessarily charismatic. Prayer and praise in tongues is rare, though all expect to see God acting in power among them through healings and exorcisms. Often there are fewer than twenty-five members in a house church — the unofficial limit to avoid unfavourable government attention — but in places where the church is strong and the authorities turn a blind eye, there are house churches of a thousand or more. Some of them have grown into churches that act completely independently, while others prefer to network. There are three main networks of house churches: the True Jesus Church, the Jesus Family and the Little Flock. Realising the danger of fragmentation, and under the pressure of persecution, in 1998 they combined to hold out an olive branch to the government. They asked for the release of their members in labour camps. They argued that while the Three Self Church has ten million members, they have eighty million and thus represent mainstream Christianity in China. They wanted dialogue with the government so as to find reconciliation and some positive interaction. They urged the government to recognise the house churches and so bring God's blessing on the land. All these requests were put in a remarkable document that shows the increasing maturity of the house church movement, but it appears that the government has chosen not to accept the olive branch. Some official opposition and persecution remains, although it is very patchy: in 2008 twenty-one house church pastors were sent to labour camps. But a great deal depends on local administration, just as it did with persecutions in the Roman empire.

A house church meeting

What is a house church meeting like? Of course they vary enormously, but there is a fascinating description in John Micklethwait's recent book, *God is Back: How the Global Rise of Faith is Changing the World*. In it he describes a house church meeting in a prosperous part of Shanghai. The host for the day, Wang, is a management consultant, and present are a pair of biotechnologists, a prominent academic, a manager from a state-owned business, two ballet dancers and several successful entrepreneurs. Laptops and BlackBerries are evident, and BMWs are parked in front of the building. The worship is informal. There is no pastor — just a group gathered to study the Bible. After extempore prayer they sing the first hymn. The words are projected onto the wall and the music downloaded from the internet. There is a time of warm greeting, the children are siphoned off into another room, and then Wang introduces the Bible passage, Romans 1:18–31. They continue careful examination of the text with lively discussion for two and a half hours. After further worship, Wang brings the themes of the evening together and links them with Chinese nationalism. The more Christian China becomes, the greater she will be — with America as her model. If you want China to prosper then spread the word to unbelievers.

Now not many house churches would be as affluent as this: many in rural areas would be desperately poor. But the passionate wrestling with Scripture and applying it to their situation, the warmth of fellowship, the sincerity of prayer and the outward orientation would be found in all these house churches which now proliferate throughout the great land of China.

The spread of the revival

The spread of this revival is remarkable. It is to be found, though not to the same degree, in all parts of China. To begin with, in the 1980s and 1990s, it was most notable in rural areas and was strongly charismatic. In the last two decades, as there has been a great movement of the population towards the cities, strong urban churches have been emerging, and the theological climate has moved somewhat from charismatic to Reformed. Overall the revival, while perhaps diminishing in intensity, is growing in maturity and stability.

A striking example of rural evangelism is provided by the Lisu, a primitive tribe in the mountains near the border with Myanmar. This was where James Fraser, a pioneer missionary of the China Inland Mission, laboured in the first decades of the twentieth century. They were among the most backward tribes in Asia, in bondage to animism and demon worship, their men constantly drunk. Fraser's ministry was ineffective for many years and he grew depressed, but then he mobilised prayer groups throughout the UK. I remember being part of one! Prayer prevailed, and in due course there was a major spiritual breakthrough. During one tribal feast, the presence of God's Spirit was so overwhelming that the headman threw away his whiskey, broke the incense bowls and tore the shelf for food offerings from the spirit tree. He declared his conversion, and so did others. Not long afterwards Fraser could report some two thousand tribespeople under Christian instruction. He developed a script for them, taught literacy and had Bibles, hymn books and devotional aids printed. Gospel work flourished and by the time the communists came to power in 1949 there were some fifteen thousand Lisu Christians.

The church was later devastated by the communists: buildings were closed, believers fled and pastors were imprisoned. But then in the 1970s an elderly pastor was released from a labour camp, and returned to preach among the Lisu. Revival broke out. Thousands turned to the Lord. And today there are some 200,000 Lisu Christians among a population of 575,000. Such is the impact the revival is having among some of the tribes.

But Christianity has been affecting not only simple tribespeople but intellectuals too, including Communist Party members. The intellectual elite suffered heavily under Mao. Professors were banished to the countryside to learn from peasants. Only under Deng Xiaoping were they able to return to their universities and teaching posts. Those who survived the Cultural Revolution have learned the hard way that far from leading them 'upward and onward' Chairman Mao had led them into the abyss of class struggle, poverty and death. Maoism was finished and left a massive ideological void, which the gospel began to fill. This is particularly the case with students, among whom there is a substantive turning to Christ, both in the country itself and in the worldwide diaspora. Indeed, there is irrefutable evidence of the evangelistic impact made by Chinese students, converted overseas, on their return to China.

But it was only after the failure of the democracy movement and the horrific repression on Tiananmen Square in 1989 that the tide towards Christianity became a flood. Self-respecting intellectuals could no longer believe in communism and were hungry to find something to put in its place. Nowadays Christian professors hold respected positions in universities. Countless Christian students are forming small Bible study groups in many of the universities. Some of the former activists in the democracy movement, banished from China, are also coming to faith and providing intellectual leadership for the many Chinese who, like themselves, are living abroad.

Some Christians in the house church movement are plucking up courage to defy the ban on preaching the gospel to children and young people under eighteen. This is both dangerous and difficult, since all educational materials are strongly imbued with atheism. In places there are flourishing Sunday schools which, needless to say, attract unfavourable attention from the Party. The classes get closed down and the teachers are fined. But there is evidence to show that Christian children, full of the spirit of the revival, are sharing their faith enthusiastically with fellow pupils at school.

Most interesting is the fact that many Communist Party members, representing the elite of Chinese society, are becoming disillusioned with Marxism, and some are turning to Christ despite the strict ban on their doing so. Communist sources are highly displeased and report, significantly, that most of these defections to Christianity are due to healings in times of sickness, and caring love from Christians, which they never experienced in the Party. According to the official Religious Affairs and Public Security Bureau in one district of Guizhou province, in 1991 only a hundred and fifty Party members had joined the church, but by 1995 the number was more than two thousand. This rise in Party members becoming Christians is matched by poor recruiting levels for the Party itself. Young people no longer believe in the tenets of Marxism. If the nineteenth century saw the decay and fall of Confucianism, the twentieth has seen the meteoric rise and rapid decay of Marxism. No wonder the government is alarmed.

How does the revival spread?

There can be little doubt that most conversions occur through the presence of Christians in the community and their unashamed personal witness. This is aided by the Christian radio programmes which have been broadcast into China from various locations since the 1970s. These often provide the main spiritual nourishment for small house churches that have no competent leadership. Endurance under the terrible suffering inflicted by the various communist purges has played a tremendous part in the growth of the gospel. This has attracted people to a faith which can inspire such behaviour. A lovely characteristic of Chinese Christians is the way they look back in gratitude to those who brought the gospel to the country in the nineteenth century. They are inspired by their sacrifices, and are determined to follow their way of life and their willingness to surrender their lives in the cause of the gospel.

In 1998 Queen Elizabeth attended a service in Westminster Abbey to honour ten Christian martyrs of the twentieth century. Among them was Pastor Wang, a respected Miao Christian who was labelled a

counter-revolutionary and executed at a mass rally
before ten thousand people, many of them Christians,
who were forced to attend. Watchman Nee, leader of
the Little Flock network of house churches, became
famous worldwide because of his writings. He was
harassed, imprisoned and died in a labour camp in
1972. More recently Pastor Yun, the 'Heavenly Man' (as
he insisted on calling himself when interrogated about
his identity), is reputed to have led some three thousand people to Christ in his first year as a Christian,
when he was only seventeen years old. He was hunted
down by the authorities, imprisoned and had his legs
broken. More of him below. But the suffering of high-
profile leaders like these, and the courage of countless
believers as they faced the labour camps or martyrdom,
was a major factor in the spread of the revival. Truly,
the blood of the martyrs is the seed of the Church.

Healings and exorcisms

Another major factor in the growth of the church, and
one that sounds strange to Western ears, is what the
New Testament calls 'signs and wonders'. These tend to
fall into two categories: healing without medicine in
answer to prayer, and deliverance from demonic spiritual forces. Tony Lambert's book *China's Christian
Millions* attests the widespread impact of healing
through prayer, which communist officials are

powerless to rebut. And he gives several striking examples of healings and their impact.

One was Zhao Su'e, a twenty-one-year-old clothing salesgirl. Spitting blood, she was admitted to the Liberation Army Hospital suffering from a virulent cancer. They told her she had at most six months to live. Her mother, a Buddhist, prostrated herself before the idols five hundred times, to no avail. But a Christian visiting the hospital told her about Jesus and prayed for her. She cast herself on Christ, and gradually the cancer retreated. When she returned to the hospital for a check-up her marrow was found to be healthier than that of a normal person. Her whole family turned to Christ. There was no church in her town but she and a few friends got permission from a friendly official to start one. It drew a thousand people at its launch, and now there are some six thousand Christians in the county and a church in almost every village. She continues to be very active in evangelism!

In nearby Huangqiao a woman developed throat cancer so severe that no doctor risked operating. She came in touch with Christians in 1991, was baptised the next year, and now sings for the Lord daily and bears witness to her friends. When she first believed Huangqiao had only a handful of Christians. Soon there were more than five hundred.

Healings leading to conversion are common in China. They constitute part of the message of the gospel itself, as they did in the early church. But sometimes there are even more dramatic signs of God's sovereign rule. Pastor Yu, working for a Three Self church in south China, records how he found people praying over a girl in the courtyard of the church. She had sustained a major fall, had been rushed to a local clinic and was pronounced dead on arrival. They did not admit her. The distraught mother carried her back to the church. The pastor took the body from the mother and found it already cold. Then he and members of the church who were present knelt and prayed that the Lord would revive the girl. Soon she began to cry. Given some milk, she vomited it up. She was taken to the hospital and this time admitted. She made a complete recovery. This happened in 1992 and the story was published in the local papers. Pastor Yu was taking a big risk, because praying for miraculous healing is strictly forbidden by the government who control the Three Self Church. Yet he felt compelled to do so. However, he wisely did not allow the mother to bear witness in the church meeting, fearing the repercussions.

One of the marks of God's renewing power regarded with most scepticism in the West is exorcism, the expelling of dark spiritual forces that have invaded a life. Yet in countries where animism is rife this is one of the most effective ministries of the church. Many people worship idols extensively and then find themselves bound by spiritual forces they cannot control. Pastor Lin Xiangao, a distinguished church leader in Guangzhou, recounts how a young woman, dabbling in occult practices, became haunted by voices in her head accompanying her wherever she went. After much prayer and challenge of the demonic forces, she was completely delivered. This is something the pastors do not make a fuss about. They simply get on with it as part of their regular ministry. Nor are they ignorant of the difference between demon possession and schizophrenia. They are quite able to distinguish the two and describe the different symptoms. Jesus told his disciples to cast out demons, and these Bible-believing Christians find that it happens when they face the situation with faith and prayer.

Brother Yun

One of the most spectacular of these divine interventions received tremendous publicity among believers throughout China and also the West, owing to the high profile of the person concerned. This was Lin Zhenying, or Brother Yun, as he is known. His story, *The Heavenly Man*, has been an outstanding bestseller and won the 'Christian Book of the Year' award in 2003. Brother Yun was born in Henan province in 1958 to a mother who was a Christian but whose faith had cooled because of the communist destruction of churches and Bibles, and the resultant lack of fellowship.

In 1974 Yun's father lay dying of cancer, and the family were heartbroken. His mother had a vision of Jesus saying to her, 'I love you,' and this revived her faith. She gathered the family to pray to Jesus for the healing of her husband. The very next morning he began to recover and was in due course restored to full health. It is no surprise that the whole family became Christian, including the sixteen-year-old Yun. He had a great hunger to know more about Jesus, but his mother could only tell him the basics, and there were no Bibles. So he fasted and prayed for one, eating only boiled rice for a hundred days. Then he was reached by an evangelist who had never heard of him but had had a vision of the boy and where he lived. He brought him a Bible. Yun was delighted and committed all four Gospels to memory — this was to stand him in good stead when he was imprisoned.

He rapidly became one of the key figures at the start of the revival, and his powerful preaching attracted the opposition of the authorities. He was arrested and imprisoned three times, where he was horribly tortured. But he not only survived seven years in prison but led other prisoners and some staff to Christ. His last imprisonment was in the notorious Zhengzhou Maximum Security Prison. Here his torture was intense. There was international outcry at his condition, and in 1997 the US Congress petitioned the Chinese government to release him. They declined. Instead, the guards crushed both legs by repeated hammer blows below the knee, so that there would be no danger of him escaping, as he had done from a previous imprisonment. His fellow prisoners had to carry him around.

Meanwhile his friends continued in earnest prayer for him, and twice had a vision of him knocking at the door of their house where they were praying. This was so vivid that they went to look. On neither occasion was anyone outside. But they sensed this vision might be a pointer to his release, so they prepared a safe house for him. And on 5 May 1997, Yun heard the voice of Jesus say to him, 'Stand up and walk out.' So he obeyed. He walked through several locked doors, past a number of guards, and emerged from the main gate of the prison. He did not realise until afterwards that his legs had been healed! He said that it was as if he had become invisible to the guards, who stared straight through him. The Chinese authorities publicly admitted the fact of his escape, and those imprisoned with him confirmed the manner of it. Although the official investigation by the Chinese government admitted that Yun 'had received no human help in his escape', nevertheless a number of the guards lost their jobs. Yun remains the only person ever to have escaped from Zhengzhou.

He was spirited out of the country and has continued a roving ministry since then, much to the encouragement of fellow Christians facing hard times in China. Curiously enough, his fame is far greater outside China than within, where believers expect God to intervene miraculously. Much of his ministry in recent years has been to encourage the 'Back to Jerusalem' movement which seeks to engage thousands of Chinese in evangelism through the largely Muslim, Hindu and Buddhist lands along the old Silk Road between China and Israel.

These stories of healings and similar demonstrations of God's power seem well-nigh incredible to a Western world nourished on Cartesian scepticism. However, my enquiries among well-placed Chinese Christians confirm the broad reliability of Yun's story. The truth is that Chinese Christianity would never have exploded as it has had they not believed in a robust biblical supernaturalism which trusts a sovereign God to answer prayer and intervene. Tony Lambert, himself very cautious about accepting miraculous claims, puts it well:

Eighteenth-century rationalism with its deism and 'God of the gaps' theology, which has so emaciated late 20th-century Western Christianity, has had little influence in the Chinese Church. Struggling to survive in a Marxist environment which prides itself on being 'materialist', Chinese Christians have wholeheartedly accepted the supernatural worldview presented to them in the Bible.

(*China's Christian Millions*, p. 121)

Certainly sceptical Western churchgoers are utterly unable to orchestrate a religious movement such as has occurred in China. Perhaps they ought to be more circumspect in their criticisms! And Western Christianity in general, shrinking like the Arctic icefields, is hardly in a position to criticise a revival of this magnitude.

How are we to explain this astonishing revival?

The revival in China in the last quarter of the twentieth century, and maturing all the time, is the biggest in world history. In all probability, hard though it is to have accurate numbers, China has now replaced the US as the country with the largest number of active believers. This has occurred in a period when materialism has been hailed as the greatest good, religion has been portrayed as outdated and disreputable, and the Chinese church has experienced active and prolonged persecution. There must be some good reason for its phenomenal advance, but what is it?

Secular researchers are quick to offer suggestions. The collapse of the Cultural Revolution destroyed utopian hopes, and its ruthlessness devastated families and killed millions. That undoubtedly was a turning-point in Chinese society, but why should people turn to Christianity? The ruthless repression of the democracy movement in Tiananmen Square, when Party leaders turned on their own children and tanks enforced the will of a government determined to survive at all costs, was another ugly eye-opener. But why should that attract people to Christianity? Marxist researchers often claim that the recent rapid growth of Christianity is due to poverty and ignorance, together with claims of healing. They argue that the superstition of the peasants provided a fertile seedbed for the growth of Christianity. To be sure, many of the converts who were healed were poor. But that hardly accounts for the conversion of intellectuals, students and Party leaders to the faith. Nor does it recognise that conversion to Christianity demands a radical break with superstition and idolatry. Opponents concede that Christianity has a powerful moral code which is attractive in a rapidly changing society and in the face of widespread corruption and cruelty. That is indeed the case, but moral precepts do not by themselves transform millions of lives: Confucius had taught excellent moral precepts but they were smashed by a ruthless persecution which only seemed to enhance the growth of Christianity.

Sociological explanations of the growth of Christianity in China have some validity but they are completely inadequate to account for its unprecedented growth. Chinese Christians themselves would all agree that it is the sovereign work of God which has brought about this revival. Why has not something similar happened in Hong Kong or Taiwan, which enjoyed a similar cultural background without the problem of persecution? There is no human answer. This is a sovereign act of God. He is preparing a great renewal of society in the country that is about to become the most powerful on earth. And we do well to ask ourselves what are some of the characteristics of this movement on which God has so signally poured out his blessing.

Key elements in the revival

One is quite obviously the astounding endurance of Chinese Christians in the face of persecution. This revival in China has survived and grown in the midst of scorn, beatings, destruction of property, labour camps, prison, torture and death. Most of the pastors imprisoned in the labour camps were released by 1980, and as they returned to minister throughout China, their courage and their principled refusal to compromise in the face of persecution has made a deep impression on younger Christians. The road has been hard. The Three Self Church has been trammelled with endless restrictions. The house churches are unregistered and so can be easily closed down, their Bibles confiscated, their members fined and their pastors imprisoned or sent to a labour camp. The sufferings endured by these people are horrendous. Yet they continue to grow. Suffering has refined the church. Indeed, it is one of the badges of authentic Christianity. In the West we have become accustomed to a free society, and we quail at the least curtailment of our freedom, at any injustice done to us, at any opposition we may meet at work. We have become soft because for many years we have encountered no serious opposition, and our Christianity has gone soft too. This does not mean, of course, that we should court persecution, though there are signs that it may be on the way. But it does underline the truth that, against all our expectations, suffering and hardship for the sake of the gospel often bear remarkable fruit.

Another characteristic of the revival is the emphasis on evangelism, particularly personal evangelism. When people come to Christ their first desire is to pass it on to family, friends or even complete strangers. Many travel on foot to remote parts of the country to spread the good news. The growth of the church has been a grass-roots lay movement. They have found treasure and they cannot keep quiet. In the early days it had to be secretive, but in recent years it has been possible to be much more overt. In 1991, for example, some of the house churches in Xiaoshan became passionate about evangelism. Pairs of young Christians forsook work on the land that gave them their livelihood and set out to preach the gospel in various parts of China. They were backed up at home by twenty-four-hour prayer chains, and so the project involved most of the Christians in the county. The results were spectacular. These inexperienced itinerants found that response to the gospel was immediate. They found that many people were spiritually hungry: it seemed that these young preachers had only to open their mouths for some to come to Christ. After a couple of months most of the evangelists had returned home, with thrilling stories of the effectiveness of the mission. They estimated that some ten thousand people had come to Christ through this campaign, and immediate follow-up was put in place. Although this outreach from Xiaoshan was outstanding, many smaller ventures of a similar nature take place throughout China. Evangelism is in their blood. The Western church has a long way to go before that could be said of us.

A third characteristic of the revival is their emphasis on the Bible. It is their unquestioned norm of belief and practices. Some of the older pastors in the Three Self Church had been trained in liberal seminaries where the authority of Scripture was doubted, but these pastors have retired or been sidelined. Nowadays they have been succeeded by Bible-believing leaders. In the house churches there has never been any question of the supremacy of Holy Scripture. If a doctrine is biblical, they will preach it whatever the cost. If some teaching does not accord with Scripture they will reject it, however persuasive it may seem. China's church is profoundly biblical. Hence the hunger for Bibles, still in short supply. And hence the confidence they have in the power of biblical preaching to convict, convert and nourish.

Another feature of the revival is their faith. Not just trust in Christ for salvation: that they share with Christians throughout the world. But faith which does not put limits on what God can do. A faith which expects him to act in answer to prayer through conversion, healing and deliverance. Faith of this sort is constantly commended to us in Scripture, but it is rare in Western churches, perhaps through disappointment, perhaps through the assumptions of society which deny the possibility of God's intervention, or perhaps simply because of our lukewarmness.

But the overriding characteristic of China's Christian revival is prayer. Every record we have of healing, exorcism or outstanding conversions is linked with prayer. It has an absolutely central place in the lives of the churches and of their members. They are prepared to pray for hours on end. They organise twenty-four-hour prayer vigils. They pray passionately, sometimes silently, sometimes with tears and groanings. People pray as they work in the fields or as they cook the meal. They pray for their persecutors. They pray for conversions. They pray for healing. They pray for godliness in their own lives. They pray for their colleagues in prison. Their lives are impregnated with prayer. They have for decades had no other resource than prayer — no Bibles, no church buildings, no pastors, no security, no place in society. Yet they have seen the greatest revival in church history progressively encompass their land. With masterly understatement St James summarises it in his letter, 'The prayer of a righteous person is powerful and effective' (James 5:16). The Chinese church has found it so. What a force China will become when this amazing revival overflows into mission worldwide. Indeed, this has already begun!

10

Fresh springs
God can do it again

When the going is difficult, it is easy to get discouraged. In this situation, one of the best ways forward is to look behind you and see what territory has already been traversed. That holds good for the Christian life, as well. Nobody can pretend that the church in Europe is not facing a host of challenges in this twenty-first century. It seems to some like ploughing through a desert. But it helps a lot to look back and see where, time after time, God has caused springs to burst forth in the desert. We have looked at a number of those springs. There have, of course, been many others.

Additional springs

The Oxford movement

One was the Oxford movement, a nineteenth-century High Church movement within the Anglican Church that developed into Anglo-Catholicism. Godly clergy, such as Pusey, Keble, Manning and Newman, were appalled at the low state of worship in the early part of the nineteenth century and the attempt of the government to interfere with the church in Ireland. They saw contemporary church life as too 'Low Church' (marked by simplicity and an emphasis on Protestant worship), too boring, too lacking in reverence. They longed for a return to more mediaeval liturgy with colour and discipline. As their name suggests, their emphasis was Catholic, and they promoted a Three Branch theory, seeing the Catholic Church worldwide as consisting of Romans, Orthodox and Anglicans. Although two of its leaders, Manning and Newman, converted to Roman Catholicism, the influence of this movement on the Anglican Church, the décor of church buildings, the spirituality of its worshippers and the theology of its clergy has been enormous.

The Lewis revival

Or we might have looked at another and very different 'spring', the Lewis revival. Between 1949 and 1953 this small island in the Hebrides, with a population of only twenty-five thousand, was gripped by intense God-awareness, causing hundreds of very secular people to cry aloud for mercy to the Lord who offered them both forgiveness and the power to change their lives. The most famous name in the revival was that of

Duncan Campbell, but he would be the first to say that this overwhelming tide of blessing had little to do with him. He was invited to the island for one of their occasional ten-day preaching festivals. Initially he declined because of a full diary. Later he accepted. On his arrival, although he was tired from the long journey, he was asked to speak to a meeting before going to his host's manse for supper and bed. He never got the supper! They went to the church at 9.00 p.m. and he preached to some three hundred people. Nothing much happened. But as he was leaving a young man fell to his knees in the aisle and cried out, 'God, you can't fail us. God, you can't fail us.' Campbell went to the door and found six hundred people waiting outside. Nobody had invited them. They just came from miles around. They crammed into the church, and the subsequent meeting, which was highly charged with spiritual power, went on until about 4.00 a.m.

Prominent among the congregation were hundreds of young people who had been at a dance and were suddenly overcome with awe at the presence of God. They ran out of the dance hall and moved towards the church, where they saw lights. And so the revival began. It was entirely God's work. Campbell did not invite anyone to come forward or to make any other kind of overt profession of faith. God met with people by the roadside, in the pub, in the church. The message Campbell gave was a strong call to repent of the ugliness of sin, and to face up to an eternity either spent with God or else for ever cut off from him. He also had a strong doctrine of 'baptism with the Holy Spirit', and the revival was marked by many falling to the ground either in a trance or crying for mercy. But by his own written account Campbell makes it clear that it was not his presence or his preaching that was the key. What, then, was it?

I met Duncan Campbell once, and I remember him pulling from his wallet a faded photo of two old ladies, Peggy and Christine Smith. One of them was eighty-four and blind. The other was eighty-two and crippled with arthritis. They were heartbroken that no young people at all attended their church, and so they gave themselves to prayer about the matter from 10.00 p.m. to 3.00 a.m. twice a week, for several months. They cried out to God for revival. As they prayed, one of them was given a vision of the church crammed with young people, and a verse from Isaiah imprinted itself upon their minds: 'I will pour water on the thirsty land, and streams on the dry ground' (Isaiah 44:3). Precisely that took place the night when people gathered in their hundreds around the church and the police station (adjoining the cottage where the old women lived). Campbell ministered among them until nearly dawn. The awe of God fell on the island. By far the majority who were converted during the revival had never come near a church for a meeting. They were simply overwhelmed by the presence of God wherever they happened to be on the island, and responded wholeheartedly to it. Work stopped. The pubs closed for lack of business. The ferries were discontinued on the Sabbath, and crime almost disappeared. This revival affected the whole community on the island, not just the church. Indeed, Campbell maintained that genuine revival should be primarily for the benefit of society, not of the church.

The main thrust of the Lewis revival lasted for four years, but its effects are still remaining sixty years later. And the key to it, as far as anyone can tell, was these two old women praying that God would revive his work on Lewis. Once convinced that he would, they began to pray, 'God, send us your man.' That is where Duncan Campbell came in. But it was a sovereign work of God, and it was brought about by passionate, persistent prayer. The results were remarkable. Five men in a single parish who found faith on that memorable first night of the revival became ministers. In one parish the minister reported that 122 young people over the age of seventeen had come to Christ on that first night of the revival, and all were going on with God. There was not a single backslider among them. The prayer for streams on the dry ground had been abundantly answered.

Can we expect God to break in again?

Throughout history God has been opening up fresh springs in parched places and flooding the dry ground with his presence. The 'living water' of which Jesus spoke has never dried up. God is faithful, and we can expect him to continue to break through the apathy, materialism and hostility that the Church often faces these days, and deal with the worldliness and prayerlessness often to be found in the Church itself. As we look back over these times when there has been a burst of new life, we can hardly help wondering if there is anything we can do to bring about another of these fresh springs.

The answer at one level must surely be no. Times of renewal like the Chinese or the Lewis revivals are brought about by the sovereign act of God. We cannot organise them. We cannot tell God what to do. Nor can we determine the shape they may take or the direction in which they may lead. That is God's business. And in our activist and human-centred age that is an important thing to remember. It is God we are talking about. It is God's intervention that we crave.

On the other hand there are several preconditions on the human side that seem to mark these times of special growth and blessing.

Prayer

The main one is prayer. Speaking for myself, but I guess also for many other Christians, I know nothing of the sort of persistent, confident prayer in which those eighty-year-old ladies engaged for months — from 10.00 p.m. until 3.00 a.m. on the little island of Lewis. I know nothing of so prevailing in prayer for God's renewing Spirit to come that I could be confident, as they were, that it would assuredly happen. I know nothing of the next step, once assured that revival would come, of their beseeching God to show them his chosen agent. Prayer was the key on Lewis. It was the same, you may recall, before the Welsh revival, with those youngsters praying for hours night after night on the cold hillsides. It was the same in the days of the Clapham Sect, with their hours of devotion before the day's work began. It was emphatically the same in China.

There is no magic about prayer. It does not 'move the hand that moves the world'. But it is an expression to God of our complete dependence on him. It is our recognition that change comes 'not by might, nor by power, but by my Spirit, says the LORD'. Prayer was so central in the ministry of the Wesleys in their day, and John Newton in his, that they wrote new hymns to be sung by their large mid-week prayer meetings. Despite the welcome 24/7 prayer movement, I do not see many large prayer meetings in our churches today. I do not see that they are deemed so important that new music

215

and songs, putting profound biblical teaching into easily understood words, are written for the prayer meeting. Our colleagues in Africa and much of Asia depend on prayer: they have few other resources. But our technical competence in the West has blinded us to the importance of prayer. We believe that we can do all that is necessary in Christian ministry without more than raising a perfunctory prayer to God. Even our evangelism is very human-centred, reinforced by testimony from celebrities if we can get them, and relying on urgent calls for decision if there is to be anything to show for our efforts. You do not find appeals for decision when God steps in. You do not need to advertise your meetings then. God draws people. God changes people. It is supremely his work. But he has graciously allowed those who have themselves been to the cross to invite others there. He humbles himself to allow us to share in the work of the kingdom. Nevertheless, he remains sovereign. And prayer asserts this. It is not trying to twist God's arm for anything. It is rather waiting upon him for his guidance and his timing, and crying to him to act as and when he deems fit.

Holiness

If prayer is one of the human conditions which God is pleased to honour by sending one of these 'fresh springs', holiness of life is another. During the prayer meetings on the island of Lewis before the revival, one young deacon got up and started quoting the first psalm, about those with clean hands and a pure heart being the only ones fit to ascend the hill of the Lord. He cried out, 'Which of us has a clean heart? Which of us has clean hands? God cannot bless us until that is the case. Lord, clean my heart.' That proved a turning-point in preparing for the remarkable visitation by God that soon followed. It was the same in the Welsh revival. There had to be a major emphasis on repentance and cleansing in the church before anyone could expect unbelievers to repent and believe. Precisely the same requirement surfaced at the Reformation, with a deliberate rejection of corrupt mediaeval practices like buying Masses to shorten time in purgatory. It was no different in the Great Awakening with Wesley and Whitefield. Wesley in particular was passionate in his call for holiness. You and I would not drink from a dirty mug. And God will not use dirty channels for his water of life to flow through. Not, of course, that perfection is possible for any of us in this life, but there has to be a conscious rejection not only of all known sin but of everything that, though not actually sinful, is a hindrance to our Christian lives.

In the past there have been various methods devised to reach this goal. Often in mediaeval days people retired to a monastery in order to seek purification. Often they wore hair shirts or flagellated themselves. The Catholic side of the Church went in for frequent auricular confessions to a priest, or the lighting of candles at a shrine. Evangelicals, when I was young, had a narrow conception of worldliness which avoided dancing, smoking, drinking, going to theatres or cinemas, women's make-up and so forth. None of these external things produces purity of heart and a longing to see the Lord's glory, not our own. But that is a characteristic which is prominent when these times of divine visitation occur. It is an essential.

Awareness of eternal destiny

There is a further feature which seems to mark all these events. It is a great sense of the seriousness of the issues, of life and death, of heaven and hell. Christians in times of renewal and revival are found weeping for the salvation of those they love. They are concerned that these loved ones do not go to a Christless eternity. Sometimes this element has featured too much in the preaching and prayers of Christians eager for God to break in. That was probably true in the Victorian era. But there can be little doubt that in today's church, at all events in the West, it is very lacking. Many Christians do not seem to think it matters whether others come to faith or not. Do not all religions lead to God in this tolerant, pluralist age? If someone leads a reasonably decent life, will they not inevitably go to heaven? Is not an hour in church every so often all that can be expected from us in our busy lives? That is the attitude that so many of us unconsciously adopt. We are dominated by the assumptions of a liberal democracy, and are far away from the clarity and solemnity of New Testament teaching. Jesus, that most loving of men, gave more warnings of the danger of hell than anyone else in the Bible. Would he have done this if the danger was not real? A man like the apostle Paul was willing, he tells us, to be personally cut off from God for ever if only his fellow Jews would be saved. We sometimes find this conviction about eternal realities and this passion for others to be saved appearing in fringe Christian movements, but rarely in the mainstream. How can we expect God to provide rivers in the desert if we do not even recognise the desert? How can we expect him to quench thirst if we are not desperate for the living water? In the Wesleyan revival, in the Welsh, in the time of Charles Simeon and his evangelical colleagues or Pusey and his High Church friends, you always find that deep concern, among some at any rate, for the grace of God to reach to others who currently are strangers to it. This is notably the case in Singapore and China today. There is a strong sense of the eternal issues at stake.

Return to Scripture

This is another characteristic you can find where God is about to bring a fresh burst of his living water. I cannot think of a single divine intervention throughout history where there has not been a serious return to the Bible. Sometimes the exegesis has been mistaken, but always the passion to return to the fountainhead of the Christian faith has been present. It is sometimes forgotten what tremendous Bible students the leaders of the Oxford Movement were, with men like Pusey being among the foremost biblical scholars of their day, and with a deep reverence for the God who inspired it. The Bible was, of course, central in the Reformation. It lay at the heart of the Wesleyan Awakening and the evangelical movement which followed it. It was central to the Welsh revival and it was the same on Lewis. In China the thirst for Bibles remains intense. It might justly be argued that being governed by biblical norms has not always been a characteristic of the charismatic movement, but the more bizarre elements in that movement have died out and the substantial part that remains is utterly committed to the supremacy of Scripture. The Spirit and the Word belong together, and no manifestations attributed to the Spirit can be recognised if they do not match up to the teaching of Holy Scripture. If we wonder why Scripture should figure so largely in renewals of spiritual life, it is surely because Christianity is a revealed religion. We do not make it up as we go along. It is God's self-disclosure to his children. We cannot expect God's new life unless we pay attention to his revealed will.

Suffering

In the mysterious chemistry of God, suffering often seems to be an integral factor in revival. Not, of course, that we should go looking for it. But suffering and persecution are often part of the human condition when God breaks in to answer prayer and renew his Church. It was certainly so in the first century when the followers of Jesus were frequently mocked, imprisoned, tortured and killed. It was certainly so in the days of the Reformation when most of the persecution came, regrettably, from the church authorities themselves. Wesley and his partners in the Awakening had to face exclusion from churches, scorn, and fierce opposition both from the mob and from the church authorities. In Cambodia and China persecution and suffering were their daily bread. Followers of a crucified Messiah cannot expect to live in comfort. But in the West we shrink from suffering. The Church is constantly tempted to modify aspects of its message and lifestyle so as to avoid it and fit more comfortably within the confines of secular society. But when men and women are prepared, like the apostle Paul, to be fearless in proclamation and patient in sufferings, God has often broken in with power. It could happen again.

Conclusion

There is no way in which human beings can orchestrate the sweeping power of divine interventions, such as the ones we have looked at. They are the work of the living God, with or without human agency, and they take different forms. They come at the times of his decision. But what we can say without fear of contradiction is that they never appear when all God's people are apathetic, prayerless, unconcerned about holiness, flippant about the great issues of life, death and judgement, or disposed to reject the authority of Scripture. Scepticism in theology and hedonism in lifestyle never spawn spiritual revival. That in itself ought to be a significant pointer to the way the Church should be moving.

Western Europe has on the whole turned its back on the Christian faith and Christian standards. The Church, with the honourable exception of the Roman Catholics, has voiced few protests against the abortion of some two hundred thousand foetuses in Britain alone every year. We are no longer shocked when Christian young people produce children out of wedlock. The very word 'fornication' has dropped out of common use, perhaps because it is so prevalent. It is perfectly normal nowadays for a couple to share a house and a bed before they get married — if they bother to get married at all. Adultery is no longer frowned on. Divorce is as common among Christians as in the rest of society. Remarriage of divorced persons in church is normal. Same-sex partnerships are accorded the same rights as married couples. As I write the government has just voted for same-sex marriage. Homosexual activity is promoted as an equivalent if not superior way of life to heterosexuality, and is required to be taught in the school system. We tolerate vast inequalities of wealth without the Church raising more than a token murmur. Thousands of children die of starvation daily and nobody cares. Churches in the West contribute less than a penny in the pound to supporting overseas mission. We are obsessed with slimming when a billion people go to bed hungry. Some surveys show that Christians in the West tend to pray for a mere minute a day, and ministers perhaps for two minutes. Family prayers have disappeared, and the daily quiet time of prayer and Bible reading, which has nourished millions of Christians in the past, is now rarely to be found. The continent of Europe is largely apostate.

How can God bless such a society, such a church? The logical answer is that he cannot. But then that has been the situation often in the past when God has, nevertheless, broken in with power. However, on those occasions, when fresh springs have burst forth in the desert, there has always been a core of believers passionate for God to act, committed to God's revelation in Scripture, deeply aware of the issues at stake, hungry for holiness of life, prepared to give themselves to prolonged, sacrificial prayer, and willing to suffer if need be.

Can we expect God to do it again? The answer may depend, humanly speaking, on whether we are prepared to pay the price. We began with Aksah's cry to Caleb in the Old Testament when she inherited desert property, 'Give me the springs.' Are we prepared to pray, with the intensity shown by Aksah, 'Give us the springs'? If so, God may well see fit to send the gracious waters of revival in our own generation.

My friend Phil Lawson Johnston is a worship leader and songwriter, as well as being glass engraver to the Queen! He recently wrote this song, which fits the theme and aspiration of this book so well that I asked him if I might use part of it, and he has graciously agreed.

> We're longing for a fresh outpouring
> A mighty flood of cleansing rain
> We're thirsty for your living waters
> Won't you come in power again?
> We're asking for a fresh anointing.
> Renew the fire and stir our hearts.
> We're hoping for a new revival.
> Please, come in power again.
>
> We're waiting for the breath of heaven
> To lift us up on eagles' wings.
> We raise our hands in expectation
> For you to come in power again.
> Stretch out your hand with mighty power,

Free us from fear and make us bold.
Wake up your church for this very hour
When you come in power again.

Given expectancy, given prayer like that, can we not trust that God, in his own time and his own way, will revive his Church again? I believe we can . . . Yes, God can wake up his Church and come in power again.

End Notes

p. 39. Adolf von Harnack, *The Mission and Expansion of Christianity in the First Three Centuries* (1902, 1924).

p. 40. Justin Martyr, *Ante-Nicene Fathers vol.1* (A.D. 160) pg.190

p. 41. Irenaeus, *Adversus Haereses*, Chapter XXXII . 5

p. 112. Jessie Penn-Lewis, *The Awakening in Wales*, Chapter 2.

p. 131. *Here is Love Vast as the Ocean* —William Rees (1802–1883)

p. 137. John Stott, *The Living Church* (IVP, 2012) Used with permission

p.156. J.I. Packer, *Keeping in Step with the Spirit* (InterVarsity Press, 2005) p.196. Used with permission.

p. 171. Michael Green, *Asian Tigers for Christ*, (SPCK, 2001) p.7

p. 173. Michael Green, *Asian Tigers for Christ*, (SPCK, 2001) p.9

p. 174. Michael Green, *Asian Tigers for Christ*, (SPCK, 2001) p.7

p. 202. Tony Lambert, *China's Christian Millions* (Monarch, 2006) p.121

p. 224. Extract taken from the song *We're longing for a fresh outpouring / King Redeemer* by Phil Lawson Johnston © 2014 Phil Lawson Johnston IQ Music, Used by permission. www.glassengraver.net

Every reasonable effort has been made to trace the copyright holders, but if there are any errors or omissions, Hodder & Stoughton will be pleased to insert the appropriate acknowledgement in any subsequent printings or editions.

Do you wish this wasn't the end?
Are you hungry for more great teaching, inspiring
testimonies, ideas to challenge your faith?

Join us at www.hodderfaith.com, follow us on Twitter
or find us on Facebook to make sure you get the latest from
your favourite authors.

Including interviews, videos, articles, competitions
and opportunities to tell us just what you thought about
our latest releases.

www.hodderfaith.com

HodderFaith

@HodderFaith

HodderFaithVideo

HODDER
WHERE FAITH IS INSPIRED